ROOM 306

Ben Kamin

ROOM 306

The National Story
of the Lorraine Motel

MICHIGAN STATE UNIVERSITY PRESS | EAST LANSING

♾ The paper used in this publication meets the minimum requirements of ANSI/NISO Z39.48-1992 (R 1997) (Permanence of Paper).

　　　　Michigan State University Press
　　　　East Lansing, Michigan 48823-5245

Printed and bound in the United States of America.

18　17　16　15　14　13　12　　1　2　3　4　5　6　7　8　9　10

LIBRARY OF CONGRESS CATALOGING-IN-PUBLICATION DATA
Kamin, Ben.
Room 306 : the national story of the Lorraine Motel / Ben Kamin.
p. cm.
Includes bibliographical references.
ISBN 978-1-61186-049-8 (pbk. : alk. paper) 1. Lorraine Motel (Memphis, Tenn.)—History. 2. National Civil Rights Museum—History. 3. King, Martin Luther, Jr., 1929-1968—Homes and haunts—Tennessee—Memphis. 4. African American civil rights workers—Biography. 5. African Americans—Tennessee—Memphis—Biography. 6. Memphis (Tenn.)—Biography. 7. Historic hotels—Tennessee—Memphis. 8. African Americans—Museums—Tennessee—Memphis. 9. Memphis (Tenn.)—Buildings, structures, etc. 10. Memphis (Tenn.)—History. I. Title.
F444.M58L675 2012
910.4609768'19—dc23
2011046884

Book design by Charlie Sharp, Sharp Des!gns, Lansing, Michigan
Cover design by David Drummond, Salamander Hill Design (www.salamanderhill.com)
Cover photograph is used courtesy of Margaret Hyde Photography.

green press INITIATIVE Michigan State University Press is a member of the Green Press Initiative and is committed to developing and encouraging ecologically responsible publishing practices. For more information about the Green Press Initiative and the use of recycled paper in book publishing, please visit *www.greenpressinitiative.org*.

Visit Michigan State University Press at *www.msupress.org*

To Audrey, who told me to write.

Contents

The Motel at Mulberry and Main

Since my primary and high school years, when two Kennedys and a King were struck down, I have maintained a furtive relationship with a once-obscure and crumbling motel on Mulberry Street in central Memphis. The Lorraine Motel, one of the only places where black people could even lodge in the city, nondescript, unattractive, with mustard-yellow and blue walls, railings, and a second-story balcony, was a cinder-block inn set in a district of flophouses, pimps, and undercover police lookout posts.

And yet some of the greatest artists in American history stayed there while making music just around the corner on Beale Street—along with immortal Negro League baseball players, basketball's illustrious Harlem Globetrotters, and, of course, the grand preachers of the Gospel, the grandest being Rev. Dr. Martin Luther King Jr. King preferred Room 306; he was shot to death on the balcony outside that room during the early evening of April 4, 1968.

largely unknown but whose creativity or art is immortal: Joseph Louw was a brilliant young South African cameraman producing a documentary about King's imminent Poor People's March on Washington. He was staying in Room 309 and happened upon King on the balcony the night before the assassination. Just the two of them. It was a muggy dusk, and King was in shirtsleeves. A tremendous flash of lightning lit up the veil of black clouds behind the leader, creating an eerie silhouette of his profile. This was followed by a colossal crash of thunder. They exchanged pleasantries, and King returned into Room 306. Louw remained restless and haunted and distressed about King. When he heard the gunfire twenty-four hours later, he instinctively reached for his camera equipment and captured the renowned photograph of King's aides standing over his fatally wounded body, all pointing toward where they heard the shot.

Many curious things happen at the museum. Debbie Nutt, who manages the museum store and is a middle-aged white woman, told me that a black gentleman saw her, whistled, and cried out, "Hey, babe!" She was initially taken aback, until they spoke and he explained that the unfortunate black teenager named Emmett Till (whose story is recounted in the museum) was brutally and fatally beaten, shot, and had one eye gouged out in Mississippi in 1955 for innocently whistling at a white woman and shouting, "Hey, babe!" (Debbie was, of course, well aware of the Emmett Till tragedy.)

"I meant no disrespect, ma'am," the visitor told Nutt. "It just came over me that I wouldn't be killed for saying that to a white woman now." They embraced and understood each other.

Barbara Andrews, the museum's education director who is African American, told me about an elderly white man who approached her, weeping, and asked for her forgiveness: "I'm sorry. I was in the Tennessee Klan when I was a kid. I did terrible things. I just want to apologize, and this seems to be the right place."

Otis Sanford has been a renowned columnist and managing editor at the *Memphis Commercial Appeal*. Sanford focuses on the city's long-held stigma and collective guilt about the assassination taking place there and the city's painful evolution from what were once conventional race relations and behaviors. He believes that Memphis learned a lot about itself during the transition years between the Lorraine Motel's limbo state after the murder and its renewal as a museum. Now middle-aged, transitioning into academia, a beneficiary of affirmative action who has more than proven his own merits, Sanford believes deeply that the National Civil Rights Museum at the Lorraine Motel is a genuine acquittal of the city's past.

Lillian Benson of Paramount Studios in Los Angeles was nominated for an Emmy due to her work as producer of the award-winning PBS documentary about the civil rights movement, *Eyes on the Prize 2.* She vividly recalls the emotions felt when she and her crew filmed a re-creation of the sanitation workers' walk in Memphis during the thirtieth anniversary of King's assassination at the Lorraine Motel.

Maxine Smith is a Memphis icon of the civil rights story and a hands-on advocate for education and literacy as the key tools in the fight for justice. The expressive and longtime executive secretary of the local National Association for the Advancement of Colored People (NAACP) nevertheless put her safety on the line by getting out of the office and walking, chanting, and demonstrating in many intense public protests during which hostile whites and nervous police were confronted and provoked. "Afraid is a word Maxine doesn't know," says *Memphis Commercial Appeal* columnist Anita Houk. Smith was a corecipient of the museum's Freedom Award with President Bill Clinton; she has ruminations about walking about the balcony outside Room 306.

Margaret Hyde is a young mother, author, artist, and producer living in Southern California who grew up privileged in Memphis, with full breeding, private schooling, and an African American nanny whom she loved. Her father, J. R. "Pitt" Hyde, founder of Auto Zone Corporation and a luminously successful entrepreneur, turned his family foundation over to many causes—chiefly to the birthing and life of the National Civil Rights Museum. Margaret became so enthralled with the museum at the site of the old Lorraine, and particularly with the avuncular and evocative persona of Rev. Billy Kyles, that she created and produced a documentary film called *The Witness.* The piece chronicles

King's final hours in Memphis and at the Lorraine Motel; it appeared on HBO and has received both Oscar and Emmy nominations.

This book is about these people, and others, whose voices combine to give us the story of a once-sorry little motel in a district of dilapidated warehouses, drug dealers, and an oligarchic southern social order that, through murder, saga, and a difficult American transition, became a national temple of renewal and racial education.

Hampton Sides, in his skillful *Hellhound on His Trail: The Stalking of Martin Luther King Jr. and the International Hunt for His Assassin*, writes: "The shock waves still emanate from room 306 at the Lorraine Motel, and continue to register across the globe. . . . People come from all over the world to stand on the balcony where King stood, squinting in the humidity, surveying the sight lines of fate."

PART ONE

THE HISTORY

CHAPTER ONE

The King-Abernathy Suite: Billy Kyles

Hardly anyone had ever really heard of Room 306, or the Lorraine Motel for that matter, until just after 6:01 P.M. on Thursday, April 4, 1968. The borderline squalid, segregated motor court and interim residence on Mulberry Street in Memphis, which had passed through a prior incarnation as a whites-only whorehouse, quietly serviced celebrity black entertainers and other notables who drew crowds along the smoky, boozy, jazz and blues strips of nearby Beale Street but who could not lodge on the more imperial, whites-only Peabody Avenue. But few had much of an awareness of the nondescript cinder-block motel thrust between weedy and garbage-strewn gullies and neglected pimp-infested streets until the dinner hour that refreshingly cool evening in April.

It had rained and hailed hard the night before, and at least one deadly tornado touched down in the metropolitan area. The pounding sheets of water and the explosions of thunder against rafters had frightened Martin Luther

King Jr., who was in town and was increasingly on edge and vocal about the threats, real and perceived, against his life. "And then I got into Memphis," he howled prophetically that previous night in front of an entranced audience at the Mason Temple Church of God in Christ. "And some began to talk about the threats that were about—about what would happen to me from some of our sick white brothers."

But this night King stepped out of Room 306, his preferred and customary space at the Lorraine over the years, to take in the cleansed and tranquil evening air. It was just before 6:00 P.M. central daylight time. His spirits, so recently burdened again by morbid thoughts and failing goals, were lifted—he practically hummed a certain spiritual that he loved, and he looked forward to a hearty dinner at the home of his friend and local host, Rev. Samuel "Billy" Kyles. Billy had arrived and was waiting to escort his friend back to the house.

King leaned over the balcony and spoke to a few people gathering below. He generally refused any security details and, as a matter of doctrinal faith, forbade his immediate staff from bearing firearms under any circumstances. He and his lieutenants had come to accept that, most likely, his motel rooms, including Lorraine's Room 306, were bugged by the FBI and/or local authorities out to discredit him. Sadly, that had been a pattern for years.

6:01 P.M.: A single bullet from a Remington .30-06 rifle, traveling at a velocity of 2,670 feet per second, shattered King's jaw and face with fatal impact, knocking him prone and spread across the balcony corner, eerily as if he had been crucified. The preacher's blood drained into a thickening pool across the floor.

It would be determined that the shot was fired from the stench-prone common bathroom of Bessie Brewer's two-story boardinghouse, just several hundred yards away. King had been an impeccable and perfect target through a scope as he lingered cheerfully at the very edge of his brief life. He was thirty-nine years old.

. . . . .

Forty-two years and one day later: In the motel courtyard, the morning air hung a bit with the weight of history. Pale sunlight fought off both the clouds and the humidity that would have surprised no one by April 5 of any year in Memphis. A small, integrated, amiable crowd of tourists, employees, and scattered researchers walked along the modest motorway beneath the now immortal balcony and the perpetual wreath outside Room 306 of what is now the National Civil Rights Museum. A 1959 Dodge and a 1963 Cadillac—both re-creations of the two vehicles that were parked and waiting for King on the night of April 4, 1968—were permanently stationed at the first-floor level. The original cars had been lent for King's use by the R. S. Lewis Funeral Home in Memphis, which ironically prepared his face and body for viewing after the ghastly destruction of the shooting.

One day after the commemoration of the forty-second anniversary of the murder at the museum-motel, a principal figure in the drama returned again to the site of the tragedy. Rev. Samuel "Billy" Kyles, seventy-six, though still trim and energetic, was seen standing outside the doorway of Room 306 along the second-floor balcony of the two-story blue-and-cream highway-deco Lorraine Motel. He leaned over and spoke to a young white boy, sympathetically recounting "the story," gesturing empathically, pointing to the door and then diagonally to Bessie Brewer's boardinghouse across the way.

The boy's father stood a few steps off with a video camera and a grateful, privileged gaze coming from his plumpish face. Even from behind the lens, it was clear that the dad was attentive and moved. After all, Billy Kyles, pastor of the Monumental Baptist Church in Memphis for some fifty years, a decorated and credentialed civil rights veteran, and a close personal friend of Martin Luther King, had been standing in that exact spot at 6:01 P.M. on April 4, 1968.

Billy Kyles would be changed forever—as would so many millions of human beings far removed from the balcony, the blood, the cartridge, the frozen numerals 306, the abruptly haunted metal-framed motel, the frenetic police, the garbage workers King had come to help, and a nation that would simply incinerate its soul that night in urban riots and explosions.

The third man on the balcony in 1968, King's alter ego, Rev. Ralph David Abernathy, emerged from Room 306 with knowing dread within seconds of hearing the report of gunfire. He kneeled over his dying friend while Billy Kyles briefly ran back into the room. Therein, unable to raise the inexplicably dead telephone line, Kyles began to let out with a guttural cascade of primal screams. His hysteria and primordial fear discharged, he shortly emerged with an orange blanket from the bed and attempted to wrap the desperately bleeding King in it. Billy Kyles also noticed a crumpled Salem cigarette lying on the balcony that King had held in his hand; Kyles scooped it up into his own pocket because King always fretted that young people would be misguided if they saw him smoking.

For the stricken Rev. Kyles, whose wife, Gwen, waited at home with a banquet of hot soul food for King and company, containment was beginning in a new and unwelcome world outside the confines of Room 306.

For Kyles, the coping mechanism, born of his peaceful Baptist disciplines, his background in choral and dramaturgical skills—all seemed to be driven by his need, his absolute compulsion, to tell "the story." He was, after all, "The Witness." He was the singular eyewitness to a murder, there outside Room 306. Thus he was able to eventually walk again serenely amid the dogwoods and azaleas and magnolias of Memphis, purposefully recalling the gospel of the balcony.

In time, he became a sort of ambassador of the assassination. He has been telling the story to audiences all over the globe, sometimes in clumps of extended travel and taking time away from his understanding congregation. From a gathering of elementary school kids in the inner city to an appearance on a network documentary, his role and his testimony would rarely deviate: "*Dr. King died doing justice. Dr. King wasn't leaving the scene of a crime, he died trying to help some GARBAGE WORKERS!*" In the emphatic intonation, one could hear the flatter rhythm of his Chicago roots; Kyles was never quite as mellifluous as he was sincere—and wounded.

There was Billy Kyles, extroverted yet thoughtful, fit from the treadmill, removing his eyeglasses in a gesture of hyperconcentration, while closing his eyes. Even in the blazing sunlight of a Memphis afternoon, there would be nary a bead of sweat on his head; he spoke with pronounced hand gestures that made up for his not-so-deep voice.

Always dressed nattily and with quiet elegance, Billy Kyles remains the doorman to Room 306. He is the natural human liaison from the Lorraine Motel to this city of ghosts and psalms and grieving willows. If he doesn't tell the story, the story will surely consume him.

· · · · ·

t was Kyles, along with the more prominent Rev. James Lawson, also of Memphis at the time, who prevailed upon King to come to the city in the spring of 1968 and spiritually intervene during a strike of the sanitation union workers. Room 306 and the Lorraine Motel have remained their psychic crossroads with blood and history. Would the modern civil rights movement that began with the bus boycott in Montgomery, Alabama, in 1955 now survive without its fallen moral leader? Would they—Kyles, Abernathy, and the stern and ascetic Lawson—individually survive without their touchstone and saint? After all, not a few of them at the Lorraine, driven by shock and frenzy and some Baptist mysticism, actually dipped their palms or their shirts into his shimmering blood that night. One or two even raised their hands skyward with the blood dripping down their fingers, there on the balcony-sanctuary, the numerals 306 hanging behind them under the gathering dusk.

Kyles himself has said that he tried to collect some of the blood into a jar, as though to preserve the evidence of what he terms "a crucifixion."

Martin Luther King Jr. generally stayed at Lorene and Walter Bailey's minimalist motor court at Main and Mulberry exactly because it was segregated and unpretentious. It didn't matter to King that the courtyard of the Lorraine, with mustard-yellow and blue walls, white curtains, and railings, was completely susceptible to snipers or even direct assailants. What mattered more to him was the informality of the place, the fact that you could wander into the grill and kitchen area at pretty much any time of day or night and find something to eat. His was a world light-years away from the nearby Peabody Hotel, where ducks marched in sequence in the lobby and refined white folks sipped on luxury brandies at appointed times.

King had long come to prefer Room 306, on the second of the two floors, located at the apex of the railing and more or less in the center of things. His roommate was, as always, his best friend, consort, second-in-command, and true right-hand man, Rev. Ralph Abernathy. Indeed, Abernathy, according to his own memoirs, referred to Room 306 as the "King-Abernathy Suite." They were something like a married couple, knowing each other's minds, sharing each other's secrets, lightening each other's sadness—although King was precipitously much more given to depression and morbidity. Abernathy had served in the army and was seemingly more adaptable to travel and sudden changes of venue. They had marched countless miles together in racially dangerous country; been away from their families for extended periods of times; been shoved, slapped, and beaten together; and had gone to southern jails together.

Room 306 was a quintessentially 1960s motel room, moderately sized, lightly paneled, with a black rotary phone, sateen-bordered polyester blankets and institutional sheets for twin beds, and a low-cost wooden desk with standard lamps. The ashtrays were filled with butts, and the air was punched with smoke—as well as the lingering scents from King's preferred snacks, including catfish, pickled pigs' feet, corn pone, macaroni and cheese, and mounds of cut lemons sitting in emptied glasses of sugary iced tea.

According to many accounts, King's last meal was literally shared with Abernathy, and it consisted of a large batch of fried catfish served up by a nervous young waitress in the Lorraine grill midday on April 4. The two comrades had tried to convey to her that they both wanted catfish; she, perhaps intimidated by their prominence, kept confusing the order, and they wound up just digging in from a common plate bearing a double order. They also gulped tall glasses of very sweet iced tea. They swallowed and breathed and sighed and kidded one another, trying to distill the tension of waiting for their colleague Andrew Young, who was spending the day in the U.S. district courthouse, along with

James Lawson, trying to stay an injunction against a proposed march by King and the striking Memphis sanitation workers.

They ate heartily; some of King's close friends had noticed that he had put on weight over the past couple of years, that his smoking and even drinking had increased somewhat—along with his intermittent bouts of melancholy and dejection over the direction of the country, the Vietnam War that he so despised, the civil rights movement that seemed to have peaked in favor of more violent elements, and even covetous colleagues of his in the African American ministry who wanted to topple him from his hard-earned perch as the leader and icon of black America. The more derisive and cruel among them had come to refer to him as "Da Lawd."

He was, as always, dressed in his ministerial bluish suit and tie—not a tall man by any means, a bit stout, with a thick neck, trademark pencil mustache, smooth skin, and almond eyes. He was painfully vulnerable in appearance, a quality that was accentuated by his strange shyness and quiet demeanor in small public settings. The grandiloquent trumpet within him that emerged, that made him larger than life, that sounded like an archangel of justice and mercy, that cast a spell over hard men and little children, that brought down the walls of the Old Confederacy, was not to be heard over catfish and iced tea and gossip and ramblings with Ralph about Andrew Young's cool jurisprudence and Jesse Jackson's inflating ego and how Billy Kyles's new house was probably a little too fancy for a pastor and how Gwen Kyles might just flunk tonight at dinner if she didn't serve up some real down-home food.

Martin was actually in high spirits that final Thursday as he and Ralph emerged from the grill and returned to Room 306 with catfish leftovers and bones in Styrofoam carryout boxes. There was an imperative list of phone calls to be made and manifold preparations to undertake: an important march was planned for the following Monday, April 8. It had to be completed without any violence because the most recent one, on March 28, had disintegrated into broken glass and looting and brutal police defensiveness. King was perceived nationwide as having lost his mantle as the apostle of nonviolent civil disobedience; his very relevance was in question.

And yet King was in an uncharacteristic and ebullient frame of mind—more so than in weeks and months—because the previous night, he had, in the words of Billy Kyles, "preached the fear of death out of himself."

Indeed, sometime after the lightning and thunder encounter with photographer Joseph Louw on Wednesday evening, April 3, King got into his bed in Room 306. He had dispatched Ralph Abernathy, Andrew Young, and the others to the Mason Temple Church of God in Christ, where a rally was planned in support of the striking sanitation workers. King was utterly exhausted, also glum on April 3—he had returned to Memphis specifically because the march a few days earlier had deteriorated into violence and looting and the death (at the hands of police) of one teenager. His racist enemies nationwide were dancing in acrimonious jubilation, claiming he was ineffectual and superfluous—even a coward. (He had to be whisked away in a passing car for his own safety.) Less hostile forces, even the *New York Times*, openly questioned his ability to lead a nonviolent movement anymore. He wondered if he was doomed to failure.

So he committed Ralph Abernathy to go to Mason Temple and speak on his behalf, not anticipating much of a crowd anyway in view of the inclement weather and tornado warnings. The fact was that King did not care for small crowds; he was lifted by the spirit of a rallying congregation, and he knew no bounds of splendid intimacy with a mass of kindred spirits. But now he slid under the covers, embracing the musty lonesomeness of Room 306.

The phone rang; it was Ralph. In spite of the heavy rain and thunder, the old tabernacle, though hardly full, was nonetheless brimming with supporters, chanting and exuberant and beseeching, all looking for King. Ralph, ever loyal, reported to his chief, as Billy Kyles and Andrew Young and others stood by anxiously. No, they did not want Jesse Jackson, though, yes, Jesse had a taste for any stump. "You'd better come over here, Martin. They want you."

"All right, then."

Abernathy and the crew breathed sighs of relief even as the winds howled ominously against the rafters and thunderbolts crashed into the ceilings of the massive Pentecostal center built in 1941. King regrouped quickly in Room 306, threw off his exhaustion, and was driven away in just several minutes.

At Mason Temple, Rev. James Lawson was in the midst of a collection for the sanitation workers' fund when King strode in, making his way up the center aisle to the podium. Billy Kyles smiled broadly—for weeks he himself had been walking through poor Memphis neighborhoods such as Orange Mound, Whitehaven, and Cordova, lugging a garbage can for people to throw dollars and coins into on behalf of the destitute garbagemen. Now, on this night of angry clouds, here was Martin again, dragging his way up the hill, so to speak, just to fill up the hearts of the little people that nobody else really ever noticed.

Martin! Billy felt eminently grateful that King had set aside the urgent planning work of the forthcoming Poor People's Campaign to have made three trips now to Memphis for this cause, that the great preacher had made it a national cause célèbre of solidarity with underprivileged working people from all creeds all over the nation. And Kyles surely understood why he himself had chosen to migrate from what might have been less racially heated pastoral waters in his native Chicago to this confluence of river, blood, and hate called Memphis. "There was real work to do here," he told me.

The memoirs and accounts of several who were there that rain-pelted night all converge on one thing: when King entered, he appeared weary but placid. Some, particularly Abernathy, knew that he was fighting a losing battle with insomnia and struggling with sleeping pills. He fought off migraine headaches. Everyone was as worried about him as they were thrilled to see him. Two hours later, after he completed an entirely extemporized preachment that fortuitously has been captured for posterity on film and YouTube hits, they saw the utter transformation of a man who, before their eyes, released his demons into the clearing night storm.

It is widely known as the "Mountaintop" speech, and people generally think of its shockingly prophetic last moments: "*I may not get there with you.*" It was, in fact, a sweeping, profoundly reflective and elegiac review of his life, the freedom campaigns, and King's brazen near-taunting of his lurking assassin at the end ("I'm happy tonight. . . . I'm not fearing any man") that consumed the better part of ninety minutes that unforgettable night.

Though their personal protocol was that King would always speak first and Abernathy would close with some kind of rallying cry, Ralph uncharacteristically jumped in and seized the podium after King arrived. "I had no reason, just an impulse," Abernathy would recall. He felt an inexplicable need to offer a lavish introduction and biography of his friend, though there was really no call for it. But Abernathy's heart was filled with love and apprehension, and it was impossible for him not to tell everybody within earshot about the man who had just come over from the Lorraine Motel at his request.

Martin teased Ralph a bit as he accepted the lectern, as usual without a note in his hand.

He began slowly, thanking and praising his friend Ralph Abernathy, whom he genuinely treasured and valued. Just months earlier, during a drive the two shared across Alabama, Martin had anointed Ralph as his successor to the presidency of the Southern Christian Leadership Conference. It was entirely in order under the bylaws of the organization and almost perfunctory, but Ralph resisted the moment because he knew what was behind it in Martin's mind.

Martin Luther King Jr. feared death, expected to be murdered, and had no illusions about ever growing old.

But something happened to his soul that night of April 3, 1968, at Mason Temple—where he had not planned to be. Roused from the depths of despair to some kind of spiritual compact, he became his own oracle, turned his life and its journey into a personal scripture (while not in the least bit neglecting the needs and hopes and concerns of the Memphis sanitation workers), and then came to rest squarely on his own emotional Golgotha:

> Well, I don't know what will happen now. We've got some difficult days ahead. But it really doesn't matter with me now, because I've been to the mountaintop. And I don't mind. Like anybody, I'd like to live a long life. Longevity has its place. But I'm not concerned about that now. I just want to

do God's will. And he's allowed me to go up to the mountain, and I've looked over, and I've seen the promised land. I may not get there with you. But I want you to know tonight that we as a people will get to the promised land. And I'm so happy tonight. I'm not worried about anything. I'm not fearing any man. Mine eyes have seen the glory of the coming of the Lord.

In his stellar work *An American Death*, Gerold Frank describes the moments of the "Mountaintop" speech with gripping detail, noting that the final, biblical declaration came "to a crescendo that swept everything before it." Frank adds: "It was like a crash of cymbals, a testament, a defiance, a triumph. It electrified the audience."

· · · · ·

Forty-two years later, as I sat with him at the annual April 4 commemoration at the National Civil Rights Museum, Billy Kyles told me again that "Martin preached the fear of death out of himself that night." The filmed record shows that King was saturated with sweat and relief, shedding tears, as he concluded the address and all but fell into the arms of his associates around the lectern of Mason Temple. He was exorcised from demons; he was free.

Biographer Taylor Branch wrote about King and that melancholic oration: "His voice searched for a long peak over the word 'seen,' then hesitated and landed with quick relief on 'the promised land,' as though discovering a friend." To this, Marshall Brady, in his touching and frank volume, *MLK*, added: "In the tumult of rejoicing that broke out at this point in the church—as Jesse Jackson, who was there with the other King aides, would afterwards report—'He was lifted up and had some mysterious aura around him, and a power. . . . The crowd was tremendously moved, in tears.'"

But over the course of time, in untold number of lectures, pilgrimages, visits, and gatherings, from the courtyard of the Lorraine Motel–National Civil Rights Museum to far-flung points worldwide, it has been The Witness, Billy Kyles, who has established the oral tradition: on April 3, 1968, Martin Luther King Jr. lit out of Room 306, walked onto the pulpit of Mason Temple, and against thunderclaps and ghouls, literally talked his fear of death out of his system.

"Martin had always been afraid of being killed," Kyles told me.

That night, rain was pounding on the roof, and the rafters shook with thunder and lightning. I remember: The thunderclaps and the wind sent the windows banging. Each time it happened, Martin flinched. He was sure someone was lurking and going to shoot him. But when he got to the end of that speech and told us he had looked over and seen the promised land, a great calm came over him. Everyone was transfixed. He was freed from his fear, and actually he was telling all of us that it would be all right. When he finished speaking, he almost fell into our arms. He was bathed in sweat, but you could see relief in his face.

The next day, he was so playful. I hadn't seen him so happy in years. He was carefree, kidding everybody. When Andy [Young] came back from court in the afternoon, he started a pillow fight. He was teasing me about my new house, saying it was too fancy for a simple preacher. He teased me about the dinner, which we were going to have at my house that evening. He said it'd better be real soul food, good food, or he'd tell everybody I couldn't deliver. He was happy.

But that night, at 6:01, Billy saw life go out of King's body.

Having spoken and been with Kyles in various settings, it is hard for an observer to believe that such a crucible has ever really departed the soul and person of the amiable pastor. All he wanted to do that cool evening on the Lorraine balcony was to hurry Martin along and get him to the house for dinner. So now he has the story, when he would have preferred the friend.

CHAPTER TWO

lawyer at the lorraine: lucius Burch

A s a squall line and harsh weather conditions engulfed Memphis during
the night of November 10, 1972, the lone pilot of a Twin Comanche
aircraft returning home noticed a sharp cold front flaying his plane.
Struggling with massively dark clouds, pounding rain, and mounting
turbulence, he flicked on all his cabin lights to avoid blinding by the
bolts and flashes of lightning. As the pilot uncharacteristically neglected
the altimeter, the private plane became entangled in trees and crashed into
an area later known as McKellar Park.

Only the drenching rains and howling winds prevented the aircraft from
exploding into a fireball.

Lucius Burch, the pilot, then sixty years old, had just spent several days
backpacking in the Blue Ridge Mountains. An activist, liberal-minded attorney,
something of an anomaly in Memphis though widely esteemed and decorated

for his legal brilliance, his conservationism, and his Vanderbilt academic roots, Burch was no stranger to exotic adventure and genuinely strenuous physical challenges. He regularly piloted his personal airplanes about the hemisphere; he ventured across Alaskan glaciers, into remote Latin American jungles, and onto sparkling Caribbean waters for expeditions of hunting, fishing, scuba-diving, mountaineering, and tenting.

On this treacherous night above Memphis, his glide scope indicator needle failed—as he lived to tell. This was not the only smashup Lucius Burch survived or the first time he'd be discussed in the local *Commercial Appeal* newspaper for unconventional behavior. After all, just four and half years earlier, in April 1968, he and a team of his junior attorneys accepted a hurried plea from the Southern Christian Leadership Conference (SCLC) to defend Rev. Martin Luther King Jr. against an injunction meant to stop King and his followers from marching with striking Memphis sanitation workers. They met with King and his aides in Room 306 of the Lorraine Motel thirty-six hours prior to the assassination of the civil rights leader.

Though this was always a badge of honor and a heralded memory for Lucius Burch, his rushed and crucial meeting with King was not likely on his mind this pounding November night.

As the inclement and dangerous skies above and below Burch saturated the helpless dogwoods and crab apple trees of the Delta region, drenched the smoky-black earth, and made sod of the cotton fields, Burch came crashing once more through the odds and against the standards. "My injuries were numerous and severe," he would recall, "including two broken legs, a mangled foot, a broken hand, a fractured wrist, and numerous broken ribs." It required two hours, and more than one attempt, for police helicopters to even approach the scene.

Burch waited in the wreckage, occasionally hollering for help, characteristically alone and single-minded, in pain and with forbearance. His mind raced with escape plans and survival impulses. He thought of a favored quote, from Alistair Reid: "Only the curious have, if they live, a tale worth telling." His cold lips pursed as he flashed upon his long-ago hunting of bald eagles in the wild ridges of Alaska—and the sudden disgust he suffered at such carnage, such plunder of magnificent and rare creatures. Dripping with the blood of birds, he repented his ways and became a spirited conservationist and designer of wildlife habitats.

He assured himself that should he die in that demolished, rain-whipped airplane, his family would honor his commitment to what he termed "the quick, clean incineration of the body." He favored cremation over what he deemed the senseless, bacterial burial of human bodies and the attendant waste of good earth—and the gratuitous, improvident, even ghoulish funeral and burial practices that came with it. Burch carried no small opinions in his backpack.

"To quickly break the body down into its chemical components, which are then mixed with the earth symbolizing a oneness with nature is vastly preferable," he would write, after many sojourns of hiking and camping in the Wind River Range and other unblemished regions of Wyoming and the western expanse. Lean, vigorous, often wearing a trademark white beard and weather-beaten fedora, sporting army fatigues, with strong hands and clear, almost piercing eyes, Lucius was as much at home saddling mules and fishing for trout, from British Columbia to Fiji, as he was defending clients in the limestone courts of Tennessee.

Lucius Burch had penchants: he liked Scotland for backpacking ("a notable absence of forests"), Cabo San Lucas for open-air diving, and the Appalachian Trail for long trekking. He admired the Netherlands for its religious toleration and freedom of expression, and the Sioux Indians for their natural spirituality. He favored marine paintings by Nowland van Powell and exalted the hands-on, practical traditions of the Jewish community ("Surely among our most effective citizens by any standard"). He carried the memory of his mother's yellow paper roses.

Though they were destined to meet, and briefly deliberate together at the Lorraine Motel in April 1968, no two men could be more dissimilar in lifestyles and tastes as Lucius Burch and Martin Luther King Jr. The preacher was hardly an outdoorsman, nor did he seek or ever acquire wealth and properties. King traveled by commercial aircraft—and his last flight to Memphis, from Atlanta, on April 3, 1968, was held up by a bomb threat phoned in to the airlines because he was on board. He turned over his 1964 Nobel Peace Prize cash award to the SCLC, as he did most of his speaking fees—while living meagerly with his family on an annual salary of $13,000.

Martin Luther King never mounted a horse, launched a canoe, hiked in rain forests, collected art, or sampled exotic international foods. Granted, he would have been denied access to many of these things and experiences simply because he was a black man living in the American South. Burch was descended from two presidents, Andrew Jackson and James K. Polk; his Episcopal ancestors founded two cities, Nashville, Tennessee, and Charlotte, North Carolina. King was descended from middle-class Baptist preacher families, and his ancestors were black slaves.

Lucius Burch sported with death; King feared it. Burch regularly sought adventure and exploits; King often sought privacy and rest and, often enough, bail. Burch was surrounded by friends and admirers; King had some of those, but was stalked by Klansmen, Birchers, police, FBI agents, supporters of Alabama's governor George C. Wallace, segregationists, common street racists, malcontents, and neo-fascists still clinging to the Old Confederacy and the Jim Crow mentality that cleaved to the marrow of southern civilization since Reconstruction.

And yet the twain met for these improbable allies in the category of social justice—they both carried moral outrage and a certain social radicalism within their bellies. They were both southerners in the blood and were both well educated with postgraduate degrees. Before King was standing up to southern sheriffs who beat, hosed, and locked up adults and children for publicly protesting segregation, Burch had fought the notoriously paternalistic, high-handed Memphis political and patronage machine of Mayor Edward Hull "Boss" Crump.

Burch spearheaded a coalition of blacks, reformers, and unionized workers that elected liberal Democratic candidates to Congress. These included Senators Estes Kefauver and Albert Gore Sr. This required some tricky and masterful political alteration in the city of the annual Cotton Carnival. Folks didn't care for it as they interacted among the artesian wells, bluffs, and racial fault lines of Memphis.

Change in the Delta was molasses-slow and strenuous; the old life hung over Memphis like the humidity. There was a certain tremulous white intimacy that bowed to the steaming Mississippi River and extended to the great woodlands of Alabama and the red soils of Georgia, from porch to porch, club to club. It danced, like the bayou fireflies, amid the mint juleps and under the twilight of secret meetings, long drawls, clinging traditions, and polite understandings.

And yet Lucius Burch and his allies helped to unhinge decades of Memphian social calcification, as well as real hardship and privation for the invisible black population—many of them former sharecroppers—who had migrated, squinting in the sun with sore feet, hungry bellies, and somber spirits, from the vanishing cotton fields now being uprooted by soybeans, novel pesticides, and newfangled farm machines.

Ultimately, Burch the pilot and King the preacher, though they were not to meet until the bitter crossroads of early April 1968, drew light from the same beam: the future for racial progress in Memphis lay in the cross-pollination of labor and the civil rights movement, of unions and the organically powerless black workers.

This aligned very well with King's rationale for coming (against the strong protestations of his closest aides) to Memphis that spring: the bold, spontaneous, but stubborn strike by the sanitation workers—the "walking buzzards" who were cosmically underpaid, lacking insurance, benefits, and pensions, and who were denied access to worker lounges, restrooms, fresh uniforms, gloves, or pay when rain canceled garbage pick-up (the few white workers were paid on those days)—had dramatically linked King's civil rights mission with his growing agitation for economic justice in America.

Meanwhile, from separate venues, both King and Burch had come to scorn and criticize the Vietnam War, its ravaging of young lives and draining of government funds that could have been diverted in favor of housing, schools, and bread.

Not everyone thought Burch was a hero for his liberalism and his civic campaigns to advance the lives of black Memphians. One of his political opponents (whom he later won over, befriended, and represented in court) publicly growled: "I won't take your time by telling you that Lucius Burch is a son-of-a-bitch. You all know that. What I'm now telling you is that he's a super-serviceable son-of-a-bitch, and by that I mean if you ordered a carload of sons-of-bitches and the railroad parked at your factory and you opened the door and only he stepped out, you wouldn't make a claim against the railroad for shortage!"

Other young attorneys, some who had decided not to pursue careers in the lucrative though often starched law firms of Washington, D.C., were drawn to Burch's fiery magnetism and his aura as a maverick and genuine explorer. Charles Newman, still at Burch, Porter, and Johnson in 2010, a protégé of the hunter-pilot-defender and a Yale alumnus, remembers: "When I graduated from law school in 1963, Kennedy was in the White House, and it's hard for me to overstate what an attraction he and his administration were for young people."

Starry-eyed, everybody was headed for Washington, Newman said, "and I was sure that was where I was going." But then, on November 22, 1963, President John F. Kennedy was assassinated in Dallas, and "that changed my view of Washington." Besides, he had been clerking at the Burch law firm in the summers, and "I had come to know and admire Lucius Burch."

Newman is a thinking man, with an understated drawl and a tendency to speak softly, while keeping a slender and smart appearance. He has worked at the celebrated practice on North Court Avenue since 1965. He is modest about his significant achievements—he's been president of the Memphis Bar Association, a commissioner of the Memphis Landmarks Commission, an adjunct law professor, and a member of the National Civil Rights Museum Foundation.

He says that he originally weighed the decision to forgo a career in Washington but states, "I've never regretted it." He has told groups of young lawyers that the Burch firm "was then known as one that was willing and able to handle controversial, socially significant cases, while our classmates at big

Washington and New York firms were still consigned to the library and rarely had the chance to go to court."

No wonder. Newman and his colleagues were working for a thoroughly engaged public advocate who complained that the South was "where racial injustice has been legitimized for generations." Burch maintained that the leadership of the African American community, predominantly ministers such as Billy Kyles, James Lawson, and Benjamin Hooks, known by their own as the "Black Princes," were "effective and responsible." He praised them for their willingness to suffer and risk the consequences of civil disorder. Burch was very much roused and concerned—and sympathetic—when more than a thousand garbage workers, municipal employees who were not permitted under state law to strike, nonetheless walked off their jobs in early 1968.

After years and years of shameless wages, being relegated to the poorest and most hazardous equipment and on-the-job segregation, the catalyst for the action was the horrifying deaths of two workers, Echol Cole and Robert Walker. On February 1, 1968, the two men rode out a heavy rainstorm by crawling inside one of the Sanitation Division's old "wiener barrel" trucks. They had no alternative because the city did not allow them a place to retreat to during such weather—only the few white workers and supervisors (all white) had access to staff lounges. Noxiously clinging to the packer walls were mounds and mounds of moldering and toxic waste—matted, clumped yard refuse; stinking food; dead chickens and turkeys; pig parts; and pet excrement.

This was pretty much how the men smelled, anyway. The black workers were never given official uniforms, and they were forbidden to shower on work time. They had to walk through to the back enclosures of comfortable white homes, regardless of weather, and lift and lug and then dump all the waste tubs manually. They had no option but to carry the stench of their work and degradation home every night.

Cole and Walker were crushed to death in the packer unit because lightning hit the vehicle, and the system malfunctioned. In the appalling aftermath, the city and the mayor, Henry Loeb, offered no words of consolation, no compensation, not even a gesture of concern or responsibility. Like a tremor, the unauthorized strike began to take shape. The department sent a paltry $500 to each of the two stricken families against funeral expenses—that was it.

While the city government postured, and ministerial associations languished in debate, a number of street marches and demonstrations ensued. A notorious incident unfolded on the afternoon of February 23 when police, numbering in the hundreds, sprayed Mace and pummeled a crowd of about a thousand demonstrators with nightsticks. Mace, a new and debilitating chemical normally stored in military arsenals, had evidently never been used before on a civilian gathering. Among the many who were sprayed and injured was Rev. James Lawson—who described the unprovoked action as a police assault (see chapter 4). Lawson, the paragon of hard-boned civil defiance who had traveled to India and Vietnam as part of his singular and unrelenting philosophy of peaceful yet willful disobedience, now knew that he had the cards, and the incentive, to invite his friend Martin Luther King Jr. to Memphis.

· · · · ·

In conjunction with King's third and fatal visit that commenced on April 3, a restraining order had been issued by the federal court against King meant to prevent him from leading yet another protest march with the striking workers. The weary yet resolute men, feet aching but hearts holding, subsisting on handouts and a meager strike fund, were garnering national attention as they walked in back-breaking shifts and demonstrated while bearing the now immortalized I AM A MAN placards.

Upon the issuance of the restraining order, the first call to Lucius Burch came from Rev. Lawson. Would he defend King in a hearing in order to reverse the injunction? Published reports indicated that Burch was also solicited at the very same time by the Atlanta bureau of the American Civil Liberties Union (ACLU).

Charles Newman was working at the law offices when his phone rang.

"Lucius Burch called to say we'd been hired to represent Martin Luther King in the case then pending in the Federal District Court here and that we needed to get ourselves to the Lorraine Motel to meet with King and get ready for a hearing the next morning. He said 'we'd been hired.' Of course it was him who'd been hired, but he was that kind of man."

Newman explained that there was a federal court order "restraining them from having a march." In fact, the order was handed to King personally in the courtyard of the Lorraine Motel by federal marshals at 2:30 P.M. that day. Photographs of King being served show the preacher putting on a dismissive smile, but he was very concerned about the order. So often, and in so many places, he had gamely proclaimed from some podium that "we are not going to let any injunction turn us around!" He and his cohorts had, indeed, violated such decrees, but they had all been state documents. This was a federal order, and King's grin outside his motel room could not conceal the reality that he was dejected by it and that he needed a very good attorney fast.

Burch had never met King before; ironically, his young partner Newman had—on one prior occasion. He and a small group of his fellow Yale students had joined King at a dinner while studying at Yale. "There was about him a charisma," said Newman, "an almost visible and tangible aura of energy and strength and wisdom, of a sort I've not encountered before or since."

Newman believes that King's energy was derived from being so deeply rooted in his church tradition. "It grew out of the power of his convictions," he said. "He was one of the few men in our history who was irreplaceable. If he had not existed, I'm not sure another person would have emerged who would have been able to perform the role he did."

That afternoon Newman and two other junior members of the firm, Mike Cody and David Caywood, would find themselves sitting, with their boss, Lucius Burch, directly across from Martin Luther King Jr. in Room 306 of the Lorraine Motel.

"We went to the motel, and went up to [King's] room, which was very small, with a bed and a couple of chairs. I sat on his bed, and he sat in a chair inches away. His entourage all came in and sat around us. Lucius told King that he understood King wanted us to represent him, to get the order lifted. King quickly confirmed that." Newman remembered that among King's staff in the modest room, which included Ralph Abernathy and James Lawson, was "a very young Jesse Jackson, who looked to be about nineteen." (Jackson normally lodged in Room 315.)

It was not a long meeting. The two leading men in the room, Burch and King, rapidly sized each other up. Burch would later say: "I wanted to be sure myself that these people were what they purported to be." He knew that his defense of King would not be popular in Memphis white society, but that was not going to stop him—if the man and the issues were real. He asked King straight on how important was this march to him and to his movement.

"My whole future depends on it," King responded, trusting and liking Burch immediately. The civil rights leader then succinctly explained that at that juncture, with the calamitous, violent march of March 28 so much in the national consciousness, his entire philosophy of nonviolent civil protest was on the line.

That was all that Lucius Burch had to hear. He was completely assured of King's sincerity and integrity: "I had no second thoughts or looking back," he would later declare.

After a bit more discussion, he departed the Lorraine and hurried over to the courtroom in order to get a hearing about the injunction set for the next morning, April 4. According to Newman and others, Burch worked all night on a defense of King's right to march peacefully and protest a grievance. It had been decided that King himself would not appear in court; Andrew Young, the future ambassador to the United Nations, was dispatched the next day and testified. Says Charles Newman: "Young's testimony at the hearing was, and remains, one of the most impressive courtroom performances I've ever witnessed."

The proceedings unfolded (*City of Memphis v. Dr. Martin Luther King, Jr. and Others*) in U.S. District Court, Western District of Tennessee. During the course of the day, King made numerous strategy calls from Room 306, shared the catfish lunch with Ralph Abernathy, and joined a tense discussion in Room 315 with a young, radicalized group of black men known as the Invaders. The Invaders, ostensibly armed and disillusioned with King's tactic of nonviolent protest, were essentially blamed for inflaming the March 28 rally that erupted into violence and looting. King was unable to persuade them or draw them in under the umbrella of his campaign.

In court, the judge announced that he would lift the restraining order. A fatigued Andrew Young returned in the late afternoon with the good news. Everyone around the Lorraine Motel relaxed and picked up on King's ebullient reaction and mood. In a childlike state, he initiated a pillow fight among his top aides, including Young and Abernathy, in Room 201.

Soon it would be time to prepare for a hearty and spirited dinner at the home of Billy Kyles.

Lucius Burch, Charles Newman, and the other legal staff dispersed, only to regroup quickly and complete the judicial details and paperwork. Walking down Main Street, relieved yet still focused, they returned to their office complex on Court Square. Newman remembers: "We weren't there long before we heard the sirens. A waiter from the Tennessee Club next door came in and told us Dr. King had been shot. It was stunning, tragic."

Lucius Burch put down his pen; it was though his plane had crashed, and the earth was crushed and the old sod drank in blood and no one would come to the rescue.

CHAPTER THREE

Lover at the Lorraine: Georgia Davis Powers

The governor of Kentucky, Steve Beshear, issued an official Commonwealth press release on June 19, 2010:

SECTION OF I-264 TO BEAR NAME OF PIONEERING LEGISLATOR, COMMUNITY LEADER

LOUISVILLE, Ky.—Gov. Steve Beshear, joined by Louisville and community leaders, today unveiled a new highway sign that pays tribute to Georgia Davis Powers, the first African American in the Kentucky Senate. New signs will designate a 7.5-mile section of Interstate 264 in western Louisville as the Georgia Davis Powers Expressway.

The governor referred to Powers as a "trailblazer." He mentioned that the dedication and renaming of the highway section were approved by

Kentucky House Joint Resolution 67 during the 2010 General Assembly. A black Kentucky state assemblyman named Reginald Meeks, who represents a district in Louisville, was quoted in the governor's release: "The Senator Georgia Davis Powers Expressway will give the traveling public throughout the Nation a sense of our love and respect for her many political, social, and civic contributions to our city and state."

In many ways, it was typical: governmental men in wingtip shoes and conservative suits and political women in heels and business apparel mingled and traded hyperenthusiastic greetings. Hands were shaken as eyes wandered beyond to the next opportunity; back-slapping and partisan guffaws abounded. Small deals were made—as they always are at such convocations that bring together elected officials and local honchos into their practiced tapestry of will, possibility, and ambition. A few people whispered discreetly about Powers's controversial past.

The honoree, though forever associated with Rev. Martin Luther King Jr. as his inamorata, nonetheless presented herself with sterling civil rights credentials, hard-won state posts, and the management of an impressive array of political campaigns across many decades of public service. The *New York Times* once labeled her "a frank and willful Southerner." In this affirming assemblage, she was intimidated by no one; her chin was strong, her eyes still glimmering, her smile broad and engaging.

The *Louisville Courier-Journal* sent reporter Dan Klepal to the event, held at the First Virginia Avenue Missionary Church. His photographer captured a shot of the sturdy eighty-six-year-old Powers proudly holding one of the green Interstate signs bearing the designation "GEORGIA DAVIS POWERS EXPRESSWAY." "It was quite an event," Klepal told me a few days later.

"Did anyone mention her personal relationship with Dr. King?" I asked him.

"Well, no," said the journalist. Klepal, though extremely friendly and genial, wanted me to know that he had covered the occasion as a substitute for the reporter who normally follows civil rights–related events but could not attend that day.

"I'm not really an expert on Powers," he said. He then offered to connect me to the person at the newspaper who was more qualified and knowledgeable about the unquestionably remarkable legislator, former campaign manager, social activist, and two-time chairperson of the Jesse Jackson presidential campaigns. Indeed, the *New York Times* once affirmed that "in her home state, Ms. Powers is living history."

Nevertheless, when I called Dan Klepal back a few days later, he politely told me that his colleague at the paper was declining an opportunity to converse about Powers with me "for personal reasons." The other reporter was not comfortable discussing Powers with someone writing a book.

· · · · ·

At 6:01 P.M. on Thursday, April 4, 1968, state senator Georgia Davis was brushing her hair in Room 201 of the Lorraine Motel. She had arrived the night before at the invitation of Martin Luther King Jr. Now, she heard a gunshot outside. She stepped out and saw a dreadful commotion, just above, adjacent to Room 306. "I actually had been listening to him talking to folks in the crowd below his room," Powers told me in a phone interview. "We were supposed to be leaving already for dinner at Billy Kyles's house. I kept thinking, 'He's still talking!' I stepped to the door to get him, and that's when I heard the shot. I saw people taking cover. And police were swarming all over the courtyard."

One can only speculate about the complexity of emotions, terror, guilt, heartache, and helplessness felt by the relatively young woman at that moment. "Someone was pointing to the second floor," she elaborated. "I looked up to my left and gasped. One of Dr. King's knees stuck straight up in the air, and I could make out the bottom of one foot."

Powers further records in her memoir that she instinctively "hurried up the stairs closest to my room. Reaching King's room, I stepped inside and saw Andy Young and Ralph Abernathy, their faces grim, feverishly telephoning for an ambulance."

Most accounts indicate that Rev. Billy Kyles was actually the one making the frantic call while screaming out loud in anguish. Abernathy had rushed out of Room 306 and was kneeling over his dying friend, talking quietly to him in desperation and despair. King lay on the concrete, the life draining out of him.

Moreover, Powers claims in her autobiography to have walked over "alone" to see King "lying in a pool of blood that was widening as I stood there staring." It is doubtful that anyone at any time in those horrific moments was alone with the stricken King. Undeniably, Powers was present, ardently and physically, and had a real emotional stake in the tragedy because she and King had been lovers for years. In fact, not too many hours after delivering the historic "Mountaintop" speech at Mason Temple the previous evening, she and "M.L." (as she called him privately) spent much of the night passionately in her room.

It is widely agreed in published reports that the following did occur within minutes of the shooting: emergency paramedics lifted King onto a stretcher and carried him down the steps and into their ambulance. Powers, who had endured the indignities and secrecies of being the "other woman," instinctively followed and began to enter the rear of the ambulance. She was stopped by Andrew Young, who, in spite of his grief, had the presence of mind to say to Powers: "No, senator. I don't think you want to do that."

· · · · ·

The weather had been challenging when Powers arrived at the Lorraine Motel the evening of April 3. She drove from Louisville to Memphis in a steady rain, through muggy and blustery air, accompanied by her friend, King's brother "A.D.," and another female friend named Lukey. "It was the only time I had ever been to Memphis," she told me. "Dr. King had phoned me and said, 'Senator, come to Memphis and help me.' He always called me 'Senator.' I knew he was very tired because that is often when he called me."

They arrived at 11 P.M. Her recollection is that King was still at Mason Temple, in the afterglow of the "Mountaintop" oration. But when she and A.D. drove over there, the massive building was shut—all she encountered was darkness and the stifling dampness in the air. The thunderclaps had moved on even as King's riveting *"I may not get there with you!"* still hung in the shadows.

Alfred Daniel King, the younger of the two brothers, given to bouts of anxiety and even hysteria, had none of the panache or presence of Martin. He worshipped Martin and worried grievously about his brother's safety. A.D. began serving as pastor of the Zion Baptist Church in Louisville in 1965. He was prone to suicidal thoughts and threats—which weighed heavily on the already apprehensive and sullen Martin Luther King. Georgia Davis Powers, a longtime resident of Louisville, told me that "Dr. King often called me and asked me to visit with A.D. I did whenever I could and I'd say to A.D., 'Look, you just can't be thinking like this. It just makes the burdens greater on your brother.' He would usually recover and then apologize for causing others to be concerned."

A. D. King, a sad sack of a man, left his pulpit in Louisville after the murder of his brother. He was found dead in his swimming pool in Atlanta on July 21, 1969. The official cause was suicide by drowning. He was thirty-eight years old.

But on the night of April 3, 1968, when he arrived at the Lorraine Motel with state senator Georgia Davis, he was eager to see his brother and take part in the grand feast the following evening at the home of Gwen and Billy Kyles.

Georgia indicates that Martin had personally reserved Room 201 for her. After checking in, she sought out A.D. and Lukey—they were sitting in the brother's room on the second floor. Suddenly, she heard Martin's familiar, "deep, resonant" voice—still buoyant from the release of his Mason Temple speech.

"Where's the senator?"

Martin Luther King Jr. and Ralph Abernathy strode into the room. There was fresh coffee from room service and talk of the injunction against the next sanitation workers' march planned for Monday, April 8. King was still agitated about the March 28 demonstration that had disintegrated into violence and ransacking. The day had begun for him an eternity ago—in Atlanta, on board an aircraft that was delayed because he was on board and a bomb threat was phoned in. He had been served a federal injunction in the courtyard of the Lorraine Motel in the afternoon, faded physically later in the day, only to be revived by his oratorical epiphany that night amid the thunderbolts. It was the wee hours of destiny, and he could not even contemplate sleep like a normal person.

The small group spoke warily of the Invaders, the young men who were suspected of provoking the bedlam and whom King had invited to reside at the Lorraine. He wanted to talk to them about how desperately important a peaceful march was to the future of the movement—just as he would explain to attorney Lucius Burch the next day.

It was late; the pressures of history weighed on all of them. Everyone was tired, tired, tired—Georgia from the long nighttime drive, A.D. from life itself, and Martin from the unyielding demands on his soul and conscience. The two brothers made tentative plans to phone their mother, Alberta, tomorrow in Atlanta. She would like that. Georgia was the first to leave and head back to Room 201.

She reports that Martin followed her. Inside Room 201, he sighed and expressed his sense of complete exhaustion—though he had been spiritually lifted by the response to his speech at Mason Temple. "Senator, our time together is so short."

Even in a moment of release and intimacy, the awareness of his edgy mortality did not forsake Martin Luther King, there in the sanctuary of the Lorraine Motel.

He left before first light and April 4, 1968, dawned.

During the course of that final day, King met with staff starting at 8 A.M. in Room 306, and with leaders of the Invaders in Room 315. King felt strongly about the need for the Invaders not to interfere in a peaceful march, given two things: First, their members had co-opted the March 28 sanitation workers' protest and thus sandbagged King into a position of extreme humiliation and disrepute. He had never led a demonstration before that was not characterized by Gandhian civil disobedience. Second, King had not only put these young men up in the Lorraine Motel out of his own limited expense account, but his Southern Christian Leadership Conference had dealt out several thousand dollars to help them with legal fees incurred by their Memphis felonies.

Georgia Davis irritably said that they shouldn't be called the Invaders but that "maybe they should be called the Disrupters." It hurt her heart that "M.L." had this further complication, this potentially dangerous obstacle, to contend with in the midst of so much anxiety and peril. At 10:30 A.M., King joined some of his staffers who were already in a contentious session with leaders of the Invaders in Room 315. King knew that the militants were carrying weapons—an anathema to him. He was unable to persuade them to serve as marshals in the coming march and to embrace tactical nonviolence. In later years, some of the veterans of the radical group regretted their position, but on that day things ended in an impasse. Historian Michael K. Honey movingly records King's delayed effect on one of the Invader chiefs, John Burl Smith:

> King . . . challenged Smith to rethink his position. "Placing a hand on my knee, he looked me in the eyes and said, 'Nobody elected you, so who are you working for? Colored folks need young people willing to lead, and I am offering you that opportunity.' Sometimes, I think I can still feel his grip on my knee." Years later, Smith wrote, "I came to understand his plan."

This frustration with the militants surely came up a bit later during the catfish lunch with Ralph Abernathy at the Lorraine grill, but Martin remained quite unflappable during the course of his last day. Georgia was around, A.D. loomed, Ralph was always nearby and supportive, Andy Young was testifying in court, King was impressed with attorney Lucius Burch from the day before, he'd be calling his parents soon, and something heavy and dark was truly gone from his viscera after his speech the previous night. There was, as Honey describes it, "a cocoon of fellowship at the Lorraine." Georgia Davis Powers told me that King "felt safe there."

Before the afternoon unfolded, King would sing church hymns with Jesse Jackson and Billy Kyles. Jackson brought in members of his Breadbasket Band—a favored ensemble of the preacher. A.D. and Martin wound up speaking for an hour by telephone with their parents, "Daddy" King and Alberta, in Atlanta. Martin blew off some steam with his intermittent, sidesplitting impersonations of other preachers. "Oh, he just loved to mimic certain preachers, and he was good at it," Georgia told me. "People forget that he had a tremendous sense of humor."

King was in Georgia's room (it served as a kind of reception annex during the day) at approximately 4:30 when Chauncey Eskridge and Andrew Young returned from court. Georgia recalls that they were smiling. Lucius Burch had done an impeccable job, and the judge modified the restraining order! The march could proceed on Monday.

Various accounts have been written and told about the famous pillow fight that ensued in a burst of glee and relief. Some say, erroneously, that it took place in Room 306. Without question, King, the Nobel laureate, went completely childlike and threw a pillow from Georgia's bed at the nonplussed Andy Young. It was indisputably in Room 201. Georgia told me that this was the extent of the pillow fight. Others report that King, Young, Eskridge, and Abernathy all lost control and pelted each other merrily and to the point of laughter and tears with pillows and cushions.

Whatever exactly happened, they would all be happy for about another hour and a half.

· · · · ·

Georgia was not there while Ralph Abernathy and Bernard Lee waited in the trauma room at St. Joseph's Hospital and doctors worked frantically on the desperately wounded King. She was not there as the medical team pronounced the civil rights leader dead at 7:05 P.M. She had dissolved into the crowd at the Lorraine Motel after Andrew Young's gentle but firm admonition about her not entering the ambulance. After milling about in numbness and incomprehension, she gathered her wits and went to the room shared by A.D. and her friend Lukey.

A.D. was asleep, she reports, and never heard the shot or the immediate commotion. Upon being awakened and being told about his brother, "A.D. started cursing and going to pieces." Georgia and Lukey were deeply apprehensive about how A.D. would handle the reporters who were lining up outside his room. They were relieved when his brief tirade before the press was over, and then the three of them retreated through the already deserted Memphis streets to the suddenly desolate home of Rev. Billy Kyles.

Martial law was imminent in the city even as sirens were wailing on and off. Georgia tried to think clearly as people shuffled about, making calls or in stunned silence, past the buffet table still laden with the untouched roast beef, sweetbreads, fried chicken, biscuits, candied yams, pigs' feet, chitterlings, an assortment of pies, and coffee growing bitter and cold.

She thought about King lying on the concrete balcony, chills spiking her insides. "You know," she told me over the phone, "his face was not torn up, like some people would say. I saw him there. The bullet ripped his tie and there was blood pooling up under him. But his face was not torn up."

She carries other resentments as well: "Everybody wants to make the claim that they were the closest one to him as he was dying there. They say this and they say that. But his face was not torn up." She continues to assert that Ralph Abernathy was not kneeling over King—a part of the Lorraine Motel narrative that has gone basically unchallenged since that horrific day that bended the minds of all who were present.

"Abernathy was never a number one-type leader," Georgia emphatically told me. "Every picture of Dr. King—there he was, standing next to him. He just wanted to be in every picture. I guess he had to deal with his own insecurities."

A great deal of inbred tension arose out of that Lorraine Motel cocoon. Georgia has been dismayed with Ralph Abernathy (who died in 1990) since the publication of Abernathy's memoir, *And the Walls Came Tumbling Down*, in 1989—a work that has indeed been criticized by many for inconsistencies and half-truths. In it, Abernathy reveals not only the relationship between King and Davis but offers a series of gratuitous details about other liaisons he claimed King had. Georgia was "surprised" and "discouraged" by the exposition. Diplomatically, she has written: "Perhaps, due to his own illness and the toll the intervening years had taken on him, he was no longer able to remember things as they happened."

But on the night of April 4, 1968, as she sat among the teary-eyed and dazed gathering at the Kyles home, Georgia was focused upon one thing: she did not want to return to the Lorraine Motel. Neither did Lukey and A.D. However, the telephone lines were awry, and it was impossible to get a reservation at any of the other places, few in number, that would take African Americans.

In both joy and tribulation, the Lorraine Motel remained the decisive destination for black folks looking for somewhere to lodge in Memphis. The forlorn three of them made their way back grudgingly and with foreboding.

"I was in a state of shock," Georgia told me. "I realized this as I sat in my room in the darkness and could not get warm. I called the switchboard to request a blanket, but no one answered."

There was no response from the normally attentive and convivial front desk because motel owner Walter Bailey had rushed his wife, Lorene (for whom he had proudly named the Lorraine), to St. Joseph's Hospital not long after the shooting of King. Lorene Bailey had become incoherent and dizzy and complained of severe headaches after comprehending what happened on their balcony. She died five days later of a cerebral hemorrhage, and the Lorraine Motel would never function or have a private owner again.

Then a second layer of horror enveloped Georgia Davis in Room 201. "I began to hear the sound of metal scraping against concrete," she said. She realized, and then saw for herself, that a workman was literally scraping King's blood from the second-floor balcony. "As he drew the metal back and forth, I began to shake and couldn't stop. It was deafening and horrifying and shook me to the core." Georgia worried that she would go insane from the sound.

The next few days were a blur of pain and remorse for the state senator who had just that year, 1968, become both the first African American and woman to serve in the Kentucky Senate. She returned to Atlanta, endured a moment of greeting and the offering of consolation to the freshly widowed Coretta Scott King, and maintained her emotional anonymity through King's funeral. She relates that one phrase of King's played in her mind over and over again: "Senator, our time is so short."

· · · · ·

Many years later, the man who managed Georgia's first senate campaign spoke with me about his revered friend. Raoul Cunningham, also a native Kentuckian, is the longtime chairman of the Louisville chapter of the NAACP. He has his own distinguished record in milestone, sometimes physically dangerous civil rights work; he picketed the segregated Brown Theater in downtown Louisville when black people were not even allowed to purchase tickets to see the all-black contemporary opera *Porgy and Bess*. Cunningham also applied nonviolent direct action in his famed "Nothing New for Easter" campaign, which finally paved the way for black customers to try on clothing in downtown Louisville stores—along with a number of lunch-counter and restaurant sit-ins that broke the back of segregation in the steamy city along the Ohio River.

It was the early 1960s, and Cunningham first met Martin Luther King during a voter registration drive as the preacher came to Louisville. "I was in awe, and remained so," Cunningham told me. He joined the March on Washington in 1963 and heard the "I Have a Dream" oration. He saw King again in 1967 and by that time was also captivated by the work of Georgia Davis Powers, who had helped organize the 1964 March on Frankfort—a civil rights protest that culminated on the steps of the Kentucky state capitol.

"She broke barriers through the legislation she got passed in the senate," he reminisced. "She became that voice for civil rights and for women's rights," referring to Powers's spirited work for fair employment and public accommodation laws across the years. Thoughtfully, Cunningham does not consider his friend's legacy to be a national one. "She will be remembered for what she accomplished in Kentucky," he said, accenting the state name in his sentence. He then cleared his throat and asked me to allow him an additional moment to reflect.

"About Georgia and Dr. King," he resumed slowly. "They were my heroes. They were not my gods."

When we spoke, Cunningham had recently returned from the dedication ceremony renaming the Shawnee Freeway as the Georgia Davis Powers Expressway. "A lot of people were there," he said. And then he added, "A lot of people wanted to be there."

"Do people like her?" I asked him.

"Yes, they do," he responded. When I pressed him about any lingering effects of her extramarital relationship with King, he was neither evasive nor defensive. "Some people regret that she wrote her book. People will talk about it, and they will say things about her in front of me."

Cunningham is content to let Georgia Davis Powers's twenty-one years in the Kentucky Senate speak for themselves. As she herself likes to remind others, she grew up in Washington County as the only girl among nine children in her family. "I then had to contend with thirty-seven men in the senate," she adds, with a confident laugh. "I've always wanted to act like a lady but have had to think like a man."

But when Georgia Davis Powers closes her eyes at night now in her Louisville apartment where she lives alone with her memories, does she not still hear the workman scraping the blood from the concrete on the balcony of the Lorraine Motel?

CHAPTER FOUR

Mighty Reverend at the Lorraine: James Lawson

t was one o'clock in the morning, some seven hours since the shooting of Martin Luther King Jr. on the balcony outside Room 306 of the Lorraine Motel. King's body had been transferred from St. Joseph's Hospital to the county coroner for an autopsy and then finally to the R. S. Lewis Funeral Home. Darkness was thick in Memphis with fear, ghouls, occasional gunfire, wailing sirens, and red lights flashing in the distance. The dogwoods wept with nocturnal trepidation.

The lights were blazing in Room 306. A few of King's disciples, still numb, still trying to recalibrate their notion of the future, had returned to the sorrowful chamber. People were quietly going through his effects, packing his shirts and suits and shoes and ties, putting his loose papers and notes into his briefcase, shutting things up with pursed lips and tight hearts.

Ralph Abernathy was there, thinking about the succession to leadership that he so desperately did not want; also there were Andrew Young, Bernard Lee, and Chauncey Eskridge among the traveling personnel of the Southern Christian Leadership Conference. Rev. James Lawson, stern in countenance, nimble, hard in form, with intensely focused eyes that mirrored a conscience steeled in morality and social ascetics, was one of those now present who hailed from Memphis. He had unquestionably been the leading black preacher whose moral stewardship of the sanitation workers' strike since February personified the work of the "Black Princes."

More than anyone else, even more than Billy Kyles, it was Lawson who had prevailed upon King to come to Memphis. Whatever anguish he carried about that, he kept to himself. He was more concerned, since hearing the terrible report on television while sharing dinner with his family, with managing his own incalculable anger as well as the spreading rage of the black urban community. He was already telling people this was "a crucifixion event."

Now the group gathered itself into a circle in the cramped motel room, which had served for years as a staff meeting place, negotiating center, informal mess hall, communications complex, and sanctuary. Spontaneously, though spurred by Lawson, the grieving survivors broke out in a chant of "We Shall Overcome"—the civil rights anthem. Hands together, they forced out the words and melody that were already part of the American cultural canvas:

> We shall overcome.
> We shall overcome.
> Oh, oh, deep in my heart
> I do believe
> That we shall overcome someday.

Lawson and the others tried to hold back their tears and bitterness. Outside, they could hear tanks and military vehicles rumbling along Beale Street. The Tennessee National Guard had been deployed to assist the Memphis police maintain order in the streets. James Lawson, who thought that a "moral blindness" had created the atmosphere in which King was killed, spoke clearly and forcefully: "He died for all of us. He died for all peoples. The work must go on."

From Room 306 of the Lorraine Motel, the word went forth. The civil rights movement would continue, with Rev. Ralph Abernathy as its new leader. Specifically, the Poor People's Campaign, which King had linked to the Memphis garbage workers' action, would carry on to Washington in a few weeks. In fact, following this devotional moment in the motel, Lawson returned to the streets of Memphis, where he spent all night visiting black neighborhoods and pleading for peace and order.

"I stumbled into my home by daylight," Lawson told me. He spoke to me from his study at Vanderbilt University, where he is a Distinguished Visiting Professor. "I more or less just changed my clothes and went out to try and organize the daily march of sanitation workers that had been going on since the strike started in February."

$$\cdots\cdots$$

James L. Lawson Jr., pastor of the Centenary Methodist Church in Memphis at the time, fervent devotee of Christ, and chairman of the sanitation workers' strike committee, had left his home immediately after hearing word of the shooting of his friend. His wife and three children watched him depart and understood; dinner had been interrupted by spectral news, and he had work to do.

He made his way to the studios of WDAI, the African American radio station, and took the microphone. Lawson called upon black Memphians to discount rumors, to remain calm, and to keep their dignity. Just after 7:05 P.M. he saw across a teletype that King had died. He redoubled his efforts now from the radio pulpit, exhorting blacks to resist violence, to refrain from looting, to stay at home, and not to defile the memory of their moral leader with further blood.

"I went on to the national television outlets after that," he told me in his quiet but firm voice. "My responsibility was to hold the black community in unity, given what happened."

Lawson subsequently acquired a special pass from the police commissioner's office, which permitted him to travel about the sealed city under a curfew and to exhort citizens to composure.

In contrast to other American cities that night of April 4 and early morning of April 5, 1968, Memphis remained relatively calm. Here and there, white reporters were accosted by angry blacks. Mayor Henry Loeb, who had been tone-deaf to the realities of the garbage workers' strike, was driven about the streets while carrying his own revolver. But the city did not burn as did Washington, D.C., Detroit, and other places. James Lawson may have carried a searing rage in his gut, but he would not rescind both his commitment and call to nonviolence.

·　·　·　·　·

Martin Luther King Jr. and James Lawson first encountered one another at Ohio's Oberlin College in the winter of 1957. King was emerging as a national figure following his leadership of the Montgomery, Alabama, bus boycott and was already heavily engaged in countrywide speaking tours. He was meeting a lot of people; the taciturn Lawson, who had spent a year in federal prison as a resistor to the Korean War draft, caught his attention.

The idealistic Lawson had just returned from three very powerful and edifying years in India—driven by a prodigious interest in Mahatma Gandhi's life and work. While sojourning there as a Methodist missionary, he read a newspaper account of the bus boycott in Alabama and was enthralled. Neither King nor Lawson, both still in their twenties, believed that their meeting at Oberlin was an accident. Though dissimilar in styles and temperaments, they were drawn to each other philosophically. King was also motivated by Gandhi, Jean-Paul Sartre, and Reinhold Niebuhr—all of them reflective, theological liberals. Both of the ministers were genuine scholars; Lawson had been elected class president by the white student body at Ohio's Baldwin Wallace College. While King would eventually become renowned (and reviled) as a critic of the Vietnam War, Lawson was highly focused on the Cold War and the spread of nuclear weapons. Lawson recalled his introduction to King in a talk with the United Methodist Church media site.

Opening the *Nadpor Times* in India, he saw a front-page story about "Negroes marching, boycotting in Montgomery, Alabama. . . . That, of course, was a big story in India, the land of Gandhi." He learned from the dispatch that Rev. Martin Luther King Jr. was president of the Montgomery Improvement Association, an organization of preachers and lay leaders who would manage a boycott of the city's bus system after the famous refusal of seamstress Rosa Parks to give up her seat to a white rider. Lawson would wind up shaking King's hand at Oberlin on February 6, 1957—a moment blazing with destiny and excitement for the idealistic man. King was only twenty-eight years old himself but already a national figure whose home in Montgomery had been bombed (mercifully, without injuries to the King family). Lawson continued:

> He and I arrived within about ten seconds of each other in the dining room. And so we visited, and we discovered we had a number of things in great common—he a Baptist, I a Methodist. But most of all we recognized that we had a common commitment to soul force as the way to help the United States transform itself into a purer form of equality and liberty and justice for all.
>
> I said that since the late '40s I had thought one day I would work in the South and maybe when I completed the theological education I wanted that I might come directly South. And Martin, without missing a beat, said to me, "Come now. Don't wait. We need you now." And then he went on to say that there was not a clergyperson in the South with my depth of experience in nonviolence or my study in nonviolence. So I recognized that as another moment in which I was being called from beyond myself, by eternity. And so I very quietly, though I did not know what I was saying, and though I did not know how this would happen, I said "I will come as soon as I can."

Inspired by this transcendent moment, and by the series of lectures King delivered at Oberlin, Lawson petitioned activists in the civil rights movement for an opportunity to apply his skills and values in the South. His egalitarianism had actually been reinforced by his experiences in prison—he regarded his fellow inmates, even those who disagreed with him on human sanctity and the prophetic tradition, even those who were violent, as his noble equals. He told the Memphis historian Joan Turner Beifuss that even the most toughened criminals were "still genuinely human with the same fears and doubts that other people have." He reminisced about a Black Muslim inmate who tried to convert him but had to contend with Lawson's quid pro quo attempt to convert him.

Lawson just wanted to teach the Methodist canon of love. He had been spiritually sculpted by the thinkers with whom he commingled in India, and he advocated satyagraha—love/God power. He had also explored Africa and was energized by the freedom struggles he observed there; the boy from Cleveland who never experienced the brutal apartheid of his southern colleagues grew quickly into a freedom theoretician. If King was about stirring oratory, Lawson walked and talked uncompromising doctrine.

Jim Lawson moved to Nashville in 1958 and became only the second African American to enter Vanderbilt Divinity School. In rapid succession, he taught nonviolence seminars, took over the chairmanship of the direct-action committee of the Southern Christian Leadership Conference (SCLC) at King's behest, and led the "Nashville movement" student sit-ins against "White" and "Colored" signs at stores, banks, bus stations, and other public places. Soon enough he was pegged as director of nonviolent education for the SCLC. He was direct, sharp, impeccably principled, and critical of "Uncle Tom"–style leadership that settled for inert change and social compromises; he roused students to take command of their destiny even while adhering to the tenets of nonviolent confrontation.

He landed in prison again, this time in Mississippi, for a short time in 1960—after leading a Freedom Ride against interstate bus segregation. That same year Vanderbilt expelled Lawson for having promoted and led the Nashville sit-ins. Indeed, some of members of the university cabal did not even enjoy the idea that Lawson participated in campus intramural football games.

Ashamed of the action by their board of trustees, the entire white faculty of the divinity school submitted their resignations. Fifty years had passed since that travesty when I spoke to Lawson in 2010, but one could still hear his pain about the ignominy of the university that has subsequently built a tradition and curriculum around his faith principles and life story.

He was reinstated, but the action hurt and stung the proud and dignified man. He stated: "The expulsion from Vanderbilt took place as the movement hit its power and its stride in February and March of 1960 in Nashville. My expulsion from school was without a hearing, no due process, though I was a graduate student in the school of religion and a student in very good standing."

Lawson refused the reinstatement and finished his education at Boston University—which was King's alma mater. After completing his master's degree in theology and beginning his ministry work in Tennessee, he kept up his contacts with peace and "passive resistance" fellowships all over the world. His travels took him back to India, Sweden, and South Vietnam—where he fretted about the impending buildup of American military personnel. He had notions of leading a reconciliation delegation into North Vietnam that were squashed by the U.S. military structure in Saigon.

Lawson had no patience for what he termed "meaningless dialogue" and relentlessly pursued talks with religious leaders of all faiths, Buddhists, third world sophists, from this country to behind the Iron Curtain. He was going to Prague in the spring of 1968 but canceled in the face of the escalation of the trouble and "my responsibilities" in Memphis.

Joan Turner Beifuss reported that one of the leaders in Memphis grudgingly declared about Lawson: "He eats morality for breakfast." Beifuss also summarized Lawson's relationship with others in town after assuming the pulpit of the Centenary Methodist Church in 1962:

> Unlike many other black leaders, he had no personal, emotional following; people respected him but they did not swarm over him. He hardly appeared humble. He demanded too much too matter-of-factly—that those who cared

for their fellows live totally or ultimately die in that service. . . . There was great compassion in him, and understanding and love, but few whites saw it that spring [1968] in Memphis.

The strike by the sanitation workers, an issue of economic justice for Jim Lawson, began on February 12. The horrifying deaths of Echol Cole and Robert Walker in the bowels of one of the rickety old "wiener barrel" trucks represented the moral flashpoint of the conflict. Specifically, the action commenced a few days later when a group of sewer and drainage workers were not compensated for rainy days while their white counterparts received full pay. That was all the men could take; the winds of rage fanned the embers of a spontaneous labor stoppage that was unprecedented and incendiary, and, out of its stinking truth, changed the course of American history.

Jim Lawson, who was incarcerated for returning his draft card during the Korean War, who spent time in Mississippi's brutish Parchman Farm prison after leading a Freedom Ride, who felt police clubs beating down on him during the Birmingham protests of 1964, who was expelled from Vanderbilt because he sat down in whites-only cafeterias, who listened to death threats on his home telephone almost daily, was hit with Mace by Memphis police officers on February 23, 1968. The police charged upon an emotional and dissatisfied group of strikers who were reacting to the raw indifference of the city leadership in response to their demands.

All reports indicate that the march actually began in a relatively cheerful, if determined, mood. The feeling of solidarity among the workers, mixing in with clergy, reporters, and some brave white sympathizers, lifted the "walking buzzards" from their endemic sense of despair and isolation. Things changed suddenly when a few squad cars came buzzing into the situation, closed formation, and deliberately pushed into the marchers.

Lawson told me, "This was a police assault on citizens." It also would become the first-ever wholesale use of chemical spray by any American police force on city residents. Historian Michael K. Honey, a premier chronicler of Memphis and Martin Luther King, wrote: "It consisted of tear gas mixed with a chemical that broke down protective skin oils, causing skin to peel, damaging nerve endings, and causing excruciating pain."

In a separate interview in her Memphis home, Maxine Smith, who had been executive secretary of the Memphis NAACP and worked closely with Lawson, recalled the day of the doomed demonstration. "The police went crazy," she said. "They totally lost control. They took out everything they had within themselves on us. It was unbelievable."

Like many of the key figures caught in this attack, Lawson was sprayed directly into his nose and eyes. Because he has always worn glasses, his eyes were somewhat shielded, and Lawson managed to stand up again after two hits. Every scintilla of his practiced, disciplined nonviolent-method inner self drove him to attempt a third recovery and stand up. "They hit him full force with mace again," wrote Honey, "so that he could not function at all. Around him, all semblance of order collapsed as police attacked men in dungarees and clerical collars, women, and anyone else in their path. People ran in all directions, screaming and cursing and crying out. Even shoppers coming out of department stores got maced."

When we spoke, Lawson made it clear that he held the police commissioner, Frank Holloman, responsible for this first of several wanton police retaliations upon black workers that spring—just because the men wanted a decent, equal wage and were tired of being relegated to subpar conditions and no basic benefits based on their skin color. Lawson even suggested that the previous police commissioner and one-time mayor, the hardly benevolent yet effectual Claude Armour, who had retired in 1967, would not have permitted such a breakdown in police behavior. It's not, however, that Lawson thought of Armour as having clean hands.

Claude Armour was quoted and praised in a 1965 *Time* magazine article entitled "The Other South." The magazine referred to Memphis at the time as "a city with an excellent integration record"—a laughable assertion, given what unfolded in 1968. He told the magazine: "I had to face the decision whether we were to have fear, strife and bloodshed, or whether we were to enforce the law. I decided we would enforce the law and have peace, and that's what we have done." The only thing that James Lawson gives Armour credit for, however, is trying to protect Martin Luther King during the preacher's many visits to Memphis. It had to do with the notorious shooting of James Meredith in 1966.

In our conversation, Lawson recalled Meredith, who became the first African American to enter the University of Mississippi, in 1962. Meredith survived an assassination attempt while leading a March Against Fear from Memphis to Jackson, Mississippi, four years later. Both Lawson and King went to Meredith's hospital bedside and then continued the march.

"There was a riot in Clinton, Tennessee, after Meredith was shot," Lawson told me. "After that, Armour hired a contingency of black-only police officers, from homicide, to always meet King and follow him when he came to Memphis. This stuff is hidden from the history books. They guarded him, and Armour told me, 'Nothing will ever happen to him.' He was an old law-and-order guy." Lawson was not telling me that he admired Armour, just that Armour deployed this special unit.

Indeed, Lawson asserted me that King did stay at other (white-owned) hotels sometimes during his visits to Memphis—places other than the Lorraine Motel, which was painfully susceptible to attack, with its open balconies and wide courtyard. The evidence certainly indicates that the Lorraine was King's preferred destination, but King did visit Memphis frequently, and other lodgings may have been used every so often.

"When King was coming out for his last visit, some white people took out an ad in the *Commercial Appeal* and taunted King for not staying at and supporting a black motel." The ad does exist in the archival record. "So he went to the Lorraine." Lawson has historically made the assertion that the special unit designed to protect King was called off on April 3–4, 1968, leaving King vulnerable and exposed. "This is what is not in the history books," he repeated.

· · · · ·

Martin Luther King definitely lodged at the Lorraine Motel on Monday night, March 18—the first of his three, and final, visits to Memphis. Lawson had phoned King in Los Angeles and urged him to include Memphis—and the striking garbagemen—in his already scheduled March 18–20 foray into Mississippi. Lawson promised his old friend "a big crowd" as he drove King from the airport to Mason Temple—they both reminisced about their heady experiences together, dating back to the original encounter in Oberlin eleven years earlier.

In fact, thousands of people awaited King at the cavernous tabernacle, and King was pulled out of his clinging doldrums about death and movement finances and migraine headaches and still feeling needed. He gave a rousing oration to the gathered throng—including some who literally hung from the rafters. He implored the people to march and maintain their strike; he was with them! Jim Lawson sat behind King on the rostrum, thinking of the Mace and the struggle and what he had learned about himself and these valiant, raring working men who were entitled to hope and fairness—and good wages. The crowd thundered in applause and ovation as King stepped back, drenched in sweat and renewal. He immediately agreed to Lawson's on-the-spot invitation to return to Memphis on Friday to lead a protest march.

Glowing and elated, King checked into Room 306 at the Lorraine Motel; his friends Billy Kyles and Benjamin Hooks (later the leader of the NAACP) visited with him. An oasis in a desert of wandering that spring for King, as he fretted about the sputtering Poor People's Campaign and his own well-being, this diversion to Memphis completely reenergized Martin and pleased Jim Lawson. His winning day was capped at midnight: A gospel choir of black schoolgirls who happened to also be staying at the Lorraine knocked on the door of Room 306. King and his immediate staff, including Dorothy Cotton, the education director of the SCLC (who stayed in Room 307), sat by in joy as they serenaded them right there under the balcony, under the stars.

· · · · ·

t rarely snows in Memphis. But a freakish, twelve-inch snowfall blanketed the city at the end of the week, totally paralyzing the community—which had no snow-clearing equipment or salt-dispensing trucks. In general, the South was shut down. Jim Lawson called King in Atlanta and reported that the march would have to be postponed. It was ominous, this blizzard, and it made some black folks nervous. Even nature seemed to be hinting that something ill-omened was in the air. Some joked ruefully that a perfect work stoppage had been achieved through providence. One of the local black pastors is said to have declared, "Well, the Lord has done it again. It's a white world." The azaleas and magnolias, just budding, struggled in the bitter cold and against the strangling snowflakes.

Jim Lawson shut his eyes. He knew this would be a setback for the mobilizing strike campaign, and he was anxious about the missed opportunity with King. When he reached Martin in Atlanta, the airport was fogged in at any rate. The march would be postponed, not canceled. They were in agreement, just as they had been that first night at Oberlin College.

The skies cleared, and King returned to Memphis on Thursday morning, March 28—after a series of air delays and visits to the Catskills (a rabbinic conference) and New York City (with some of his key funders). He was sleep-deprived, agitated, and temperamental. The ensuing day in Memphis would only send him to the depths of despair and uncertainty.

James Lawson was marshal of the protest march, which had been rescheduled after the curious snowstorm of the previous week. King and his immediate lieutenants were placed at the front of the march. It was a warm day. King clearly looked apprehensive from the outset. There was no ongoing communication between those at the forefront of the march, which involved hundreds of people under various jurisdictions, and the rear. Basically, King, who had arrived late, was plopped down at the front of a large, unruly, unprompted throng of people who were not in any kind of sync. Some reports indicated that King's eyes were glazed and that, in his stupor, he was more or less led along by others at the helm.

King flinched, clearly frightened, when windows were heard cracking suddenly behind him. Glass shattered, and thrown bricks hit walls and embankments as a riot broke out in the rear sections of the "march." Young kids ran up and down the path of the march, meant to be classically peaceful and Gandhian, shouting "Burn, baby, burn!" King, his eyes blank with fear and disbelief, was walking through his worst nightmare. Some people thought King's life was in real danger—even as police inexplicably stood by while hoodlums broke up storefronts and looted and rampaged. Police began to swing their clubs and again sprayed Mace. It was a full-sprung ruckus; citizens were pummeled by police helter-skelter.

James Lawson somehow obtained a bullhorn and exhorted people in front to stop walking. He got word to Ralph Abernathy that King had to be gotten out of there, now! King had the presence of mind to initially refuse, worried that people would say he ran away. (They did say that in the aftermath.) A passing car was flagged down, and King was thrown in. Bernard Lee took the wheel and drove to the Holiday Inn Rivermont Hotel, where King was given sanctuary. There he retired to the back bedroom of the suite and eventually fell into a blue sleep. Never had he been so dejected and defeated.

Bernard Lee, one of King's closest faithful, died in 1991. He made a statement for the award-winning television series *Eyes on the Prize* about that moment in Memphis:

> We went to the motel. [King] didn't say anything. He just asked where was Jim, Jim Lawson. Jim, I'm sure, was out there trying to deal with the march. . . . But he just, he got on the bed and just rested, just went to sleep. I recall Ralph Abernathy getting a spread and putting it over him, and he just slept through it. He just slept. He slept his discontent off. But I knew he was terribly, terribly moved, terribly upset by the events of this march, because deep in his heart and his mind, he knew that he would be criticized for the violent outburst of the march.

James Lawson told me in 2010, with the anger still in his throat: "This was a police attack." And indeed, Lawson stayed with the march until it finally dispersed and the police pulled back, and people, some bleeding and cut, others bludgeoned or gassed, others simply horrified, got home or to the nearest church. The day was truly a disaster for King and for the Poor People's Campaign he was trying to organize, and it was more or less a coda in the history of the nonviolent civil rights movement of the 1960s.

Though the bedlam was partially the result of outside agitators in the black community, including the Invaders, and was stoked by the police, it remains the only march that King ever led in his short life that culminated in violence. Jim Lawson confirmed for me that, in the aftermath, King just wanted to get out of Memphis.

And, again, it was Lawson who was left behind to preserve some kind of détente in the city, even while maintaining the sanitation work stoppage that had begun February 12. Lawson repeated to me: "My responsibility was to hold the black community in unity."

It was during those most turbulent and polarizing days and weeks that an unlikely friendship began to develop—between Rev. Lawson and a prominent white businessman and city trailblazer named John T. Fisher. Fisher, a prosperous car dealer and active Rotarian, lived next door to Memphis mayor Henry Loeb—making it all the more improbable that he would come to partner in any way with Lawson. Loeb would simply not recognize the sanitation workers' union, and Lawson was the much-feared, even hated black personification of the labor campaign.

Fisher had a strain of conscience, however. He was drawn to Lawson's fierce advocacy of the "walking buzzards," and he was driven by deeply held Christian beliefs. Even before the April 4 assassination of King, Fisher began to quietly meet and interact with Lawson. In 2010, Fisher told me from his Memphis home: "He was a whole person. There was no imagery with Jim Lawson." Fisher attempted to speak to his neighbor Henry Loeb about the growing disorder in Memphis—as an entrepreneur, he certainly believed that the deadlocked situation could only damage the fiscal health and reputation of the city.

Mayor Loeb did not listen to anyone who even implied there should be an accommodation with the black garbage workers. Fisher's growing admiration for Jim Lawson, his speeches, his moral obduracy, and his unwavering physical and spiritual commitment to his cause led Fisher to a gnawing struggle with his own social codes. "Finally, I couldn't waffle," he told me. Fisher broke with his circle of Episcopalian power brokers and spoke of reconciliation and a settlement with the strikers.

"Why?" I asked him. "What so impassioned you to their cause?"

Fisher's answer was quiet but direct: "I guess I remembered what I learned in Sunday school." In a 2008 interview with *Memphis* magazine, Fisher recalled his meetings with Lawson during the brunt of the crisis. Fisher sometimes brought one or two other sympathetic whites. "Jim told us that we were the only group of white people to go see him about [the strike] and not tell him what to do. We went and we listened. We became good friends then, and have stayed that way. I would see Jim in those days more often than I would Henry Loeb. I'd go places and he'd be surprised to see me. But that's how our friendship grew."

On the day after the assassination at the Lorraine Motel, Fisher found himself at the R. S. Lewis Funeral Home—one of very few whites there or even out and about at all in the city. "I didn't know what to expect, but I was sitting in the chapel when an open casket was rolled into the room, with Martin Luther King in it. I remember looking at it and thinking to myself: John T., you could have met him so easily, and now you can't. It was a very profound feeling, standing there, looking at that."

Fisher formed a group called Memphis Cares. He organized a reconciliation rally at Crump Stadium for April 7, Palm Sunday—9,000 people appeared, and the crowd was thoroughly mixed racially. Lawson spoke and was characteristically direct and frank, challenging the crowd to do more than just talk and pontificate. His fresh, unbridled grief for Martin took hold of him, and he berated the city for creating the atmosphere for "a crucifixion here in Memphis." Fisher was initially worried that Lawson's rhetoric might only inflame the situation, but he soon came to esteem this moment as well.

John T. Fisher suffered for his actions; he was ostracized by other whites and, in his own words to me, "experienced some turmoil in my life." He said that men forbade their wives to come to the Fisher home in the aftermath of his Memphis Cares endeavors. One woman who grew up in the city amid the white elite told me that the Fishers were banished and went bankrupt. In fact, John took his family and moved to Geneva, where he spent several years rebuilding his life and his capital. Today, long returned home, he is regarded in Memphis as one of "the lions" of that terrible era when police maced civilians, when children were told not to mingle with black people, and when men went mad.

I asked Rev. Lawson about his alliance with John T. Fisher. "Oh, yes," he said, his tone softening with affection. "We met for the first time very late at night at the Peabody Hotel," implying the veil of secrecy that had to attend such a rendezvous in that hotel. "There was in him that which touched what was in me."

Lawson added, "You know, he was one of the prized young men of white Memphis. But he saw a different light, and we were very much drawn together. I think it was his strong roots in the church that sent him back to those good values."

"I guess I just remembered what I learned in Sunday school," John T. Fisher reiterated.

$$\cdot \ \cdot \ \cdot \ \cdot \ \cdot$$

April 3: Martin Luther King Jr. returned to Memphis. When he gathered himself up from the Lorraine Motel that evening, and responded to Ralph Abernathy's call from Mason Temple to "come over" and speak, James Lawson was in the hall. The ever-present Lawson was collecting donations for the strikers' fund with an open garbage pail in his hands. When King began to speak, and the long discourse of the "mountaintop" unfolded with the thunderclaps of that night, Jim slipped out of sight. He listened, growing transfixed, sensing something almost otherworldly in Martin's weary but dedicated cadence, from a hidden spot in the back of the hall. In time, King's dark brilliance that night, his cryptic struggle dancing against the stark prophecy of his impending death, drew Lawson out of the shadows and into the congregational pews. He stood in wonder and trepidation.

Years later, even when Lawson and his wife, Dorothy, and their children found some peace and contentment as he led the Holman Methodist Church in Los Angeles, Lawson's grief for Martin would get the better of him. But never in public—that was his pledge. He'd have trouble sleeping, he'd bury himself in holy books, he'd just break down, remove his glasses, and cry his heart out. King had so often teased him about being a Methodist, an "outsider" among the Baptist inner clique. But Lawson and King were of the same ideology, wavelength, and conviction. They were intellectual brothers.

I asked James Lawson about the Lorraine Motel. He really did not want to discuss it. With some brusqueness, he said, "I really have only been there once since . . . since then. My wife and I toured the museum, but that was it."

Today, the leadership of the National Civil Rights Museum at the Lorraine Motel continues to be baffled and frustrated by James Lawson's disengagement from the site. Beverly Robertson, the president and executive director, has shared with me that "we have got a find a way to get Jim Lawson in here—he was so much part of what happened in Memphis in 1968." Robertson is exactly right about Lawson's monumental role in the sanitation workers' strike and the recruitment of Martin Luther King Jr. into the fray.

Perhaps he still hears Gandhi whispering in his ear and just needs to spin his yarn in silence.

PART TWO

THE TRANSITION

CHAPTER FIVE

Breaking the Barriers: Maxine Smith

axine Smith, the ebullient and resolute executive secretary of the Memphis NAACP, was late for dinner at Gwen and Billy Kyles's home on April 4, 1968. In her car were two visiting law students from out of town—they were planning to observe the projected sanitation workers' march on Monday, April 8, to be led by Martin Luther King Jr. King, of course, was to be the guest of honor at dinner.

The streets were emptying, now just past 6:00 p.m., and a strange sense of trouble and trepidation pervaded the air. Maxine noticed a police vehicle, red light flashing and siren screaming, clearly speeding in the direction of the Lorraine Motel. Thinking with chills about her little boy, Smitty, who was at home with her husband, Vasco, Maxine nonetheless turned her car in the direction of the motel on Mulberry Street.

"Everybody was always thinking about Dr. King and how he was doing, and thinking about the Lorraine, whenever he was in town," she told me when I visited with her in her home.

She said she was hardly alone that Thursday evening in 1968 when focusing, with alarm, upon the Lorraine Motel. Word of the shooting of King was spreading fast, and a slew of activists, sanitation union officials, King staff, panicked acolytes, reporters, and law officials were heading in that direction. The vast majority would not gain access to the site—Memphis police quickly cordoned off the area. "You couldn't get by them, no way," she said.

Maxine recalls that she observed a young man named John Henry Ferguson as she neared the motel. She slammed on her brakes and shouted out to Ferguson. The unfortunate young man had been continuously harassed and physically roughed up by the police over the course of the sanitation strike that spring. He was running so fast that, according to historian Michael K. Honey, "his shoes had come off, and he was carrying them."

It was a night of frightened people, scuttling in all directions, having lost their shoes and their minds. Maxine, however, steeled by years of nonviolent protest, jailing, and thrashing, remained steadfast. "John Henry, what's wrong with you?" she demanded to know.

"They shot Dr. King! They shot Dr. King!" he blurted out. Maxine remembered that he repeated the phrase.

"Get in the car, John Henry," she commanded, immediately concerned that if the police caught him, especially given the news, they would resume their habitual beating and arresting of the luckless man. "I knew he wasn't supposed to be out once it was getting dark," she emphasized.

Maxine Smith was unable to traverse the police barricades at the cusp of the Lorraine Motel. She remembers just running about, in shock and horror, after parking her car nearby. She again thought of her little boy, Smitty, and resolved to get home—there could be serious rioting through the night. The two white law students she had carted remained at the scene. They were arrested by the police as the first two suspects in the assassination of King, only to be released hours later after a local black attorney pleaded for them at headquarters.

Meanwhile, Martin was shot dead at the Lorraine Motel! Maxine's heart pounded with disbelief and dismay. She recalled this in 2010, as we sat together in her Memphis living room. Her son, Smitty, served us coffee, chicken salad, filet slices, and cornbread while maintaining attentive eyes on his mother. Maxine was reminiscing. She conceded that, though a normally composed and unruffled schoolteacher and NAACP leader, she had gone delirious for a few moments on April 4, 1968—somewhere in the gathering and ghastly shadows of the Lorraine Motel, against the red lights of police and ambulance vehicles and in the mounting shrill of peril.

A thought flashed in her head of Martin, when he was only sixteen years old and already an undergraduate at Morehouse College. She was a rambunctious, fun-loving student herself at the nearby all-girls Spelman College—in her word, "flirtatious." She chased boys and played jacks through the night—she herself was only fifteen and, like the very studious Martin, a bit of a wunderkind. "He was a nerd," she said. The nerd went on to earn a Ph.D. at Boston University, and she graduated in 1949 with an honors degree in biology. Her parents, well aware that Tennessee did not welcome African Americans into its schools of higher education, managed somehow to get her into Middlebury College in Vermont, where she completed a master's degree in French. Even in Vermont, she endured racial slurs and housing discrimination and the innate sense of being different and unwanted. It made Maxine angry—and she turned the rage into social action for the rest of her life.

But on this dreadful night of April 4, Maxine girded and steeled herself: she had to get home to her then eleven-year-old boy. "Once I got my head cleared up again," she told me, "I knew that's what I had to do—get home. I didn't know if the lady who watched him was still there or not. My husband, Vasco, was still at the office, so I was very concerned about my boy." Vasco Smith, a dentist and former Shelby County commissioner who died in 2009, was a renowned community rights leader as well; they had been life partners in every category for over fifty years. He had brimmed with pride when Maxine won the Freedom Award from the National Civil Rights Museum, along with President Bill Clinton, in 2003.

Their son, Smitty, had just been with her the previous night, in 1968, and saw King, up close, at Mason Temple, and heard the terribly prophetic "Mountaintop" speech. She feared that Smitty might turn on the television at home and suffer through the reports of the killing and the predictable violence that would ensue in the city. Her grown son, who now retrieves her faxes and email ("My eyes, they are failing me," she told me), remembers that the night of April 4, 1968, was more endurable because Maxine did make it home before he became aware of the news. "I'm glad my son lived through those times," Maxine declared.

Joining us that afternoon, along with my wife, Audrey, was Maxine's pastor, Rev. Roslyn Nichols, a diminutive yet glowing presence, a cheerful and informal younger woman in jeans and good spirits who had performed the memorial service for Dr. Vasco Smith exactly one year earlier. She chimed in, "Maxine, you took Smitty everywhere!" And "everywhere" in the 1960s and 1970s, for Maxine Smith, included protest marches, sit-ins, picket lines, school board election campaigns, rallies at Mason Temple, meetings at the Lorraine Motel, and, from time to time, jail cells.

At one point in the visit, Smitty, now a soft and kind man in his early fifties, put in the famed DVD presentation in the large screen Vizio unit about their friend Billy Kyles, entitled *The Witness*. The piece had just been nominated for an Emmy award (having previously garnered an Academy Award nomination), and it features Smith, Kyles, and the late Rev. Benjamin Hooks offering extended interviews and commentaries about King and his last hours and moments at the Lorraine Motel. Smitty wanted us to see a certain clip in the documentary in which he is clearly visible—a beaming eleven-year-old boy—among a group of adults standing by as King makes a statement to the press in Memphis sometime in 1968.

· · · · ·

Maxine Smith is well acquainted with turbulence and violence affecting her and her friends. She and Vasco spearheaded an unprecedented voter registration campaign for black Memphians beginning in the late 1950s. In one extended effort, defying police hostility, the physical assaults of white supremacists, routine death threats, and personal humiliations (in one instance, police detained her for hours in a men's urinal), they raised the number of registered black voters from 10,000 to over 50,000. Of such efforts, Maxine told me over and over again: "Oh, I didn't do that much. Other people did it, and I was just there." When we walked through her home and I took in her wall after wall of plaques, honors, and awards, she routinely dismissed all the notoriety, mentioning the names and sacrifices of others who brought about this change or that and saying, "I was lucky enough to be there, that's all."

But this lifelong refrain, genuine and affecting, simply defies the truth. Maxine spent decades knocking on doors, speaking at churches, visiting social clubs and Greek letter organizations, being handled, pushed, and arrested by sheriffs and city police officers. Young Smitty was recruited to pass out handbills in one neighborhood after another, approaching polling booths but keeping a safe distance at the same time. He was arrested often enough and says, "They tried to scare me pretty good."

Maxine herself felt scared when her friend and "kindred spirit" Medgar Evers was killed in cold blood in front of his Jackson, Mississippi, home in 1963. Evers had served in Europe during World War II, as had Vasco Smith, in a segregated unit. He was indignant that he fought as an American to free French and German citizens from the fascists, but returned to an America where he was summarily humiliated, blocked, beaten, spat upon, and, specifically, barred from entering the University of Mississippi law school. He was quoted as saying, prophetically in his case: "Now after the Germans and the Japanese hadn't killed us, it looked as though white Mississippians would."

Now Maxine, normally upbeat and bubbly, even when recollecting difficult events, leaned forward. Her face tightened as she spoke about the murder of Medgar Evers. "Vasco was invited to speak at one of their voter registration and desegregation rallies down there. They were doing what we were doing here in Memphis—trying to get black people to vote. But Medgar, he was so tired, so weak from all the endless picketing and marching, the beatings, and the fire bombings. They had already thrown bombs at his house. He was like bones—I hand-fed him ice cream and kept trying to encourage him."

There was profound pain in Smith's face now as she relived the night of June 12, 1963. "We were at a little country church. I never saw a more spirited rally. I just felt such admiration for Medgar. He never stopped working for the cause, day in and day out. We at the NAACP had a little reception for him after the church service. Billy Kyles was there, too. He was one of the leaders who came over from Memphis and spoke at the nightly mass meetings. But Medgar, he was exhausted, and I was totally overwhelmed by him. I went over to him and just hugged him. I hugged him so hard. I kissed him goodnight. You know, I was flirtatious in those days because I still could be. [She allowed a little laugh to escape.] But I was not flirting. It was a spiritual feeling. I told him not to let them stop him, not to let anything stop him. There was just a huge emotional feeling I had."

Moments later, she said, "We were giggling, a girlfriend and I. We were hanging out in these big old cars we had for some reason. One was a black Cadillac and the other was white. I remember that Billy Kyles told us, 'You know someone might kill you for having those cars.' But we just giggled. Then all of a sudden, Vasco comes out and he's telling us, 'They shot Medgar.' It was so terrible. So awful. I felt the worst I can ever remember."

Evers had gone home to his wife, Myrlie, and his children. Maxine Smith was the last person to embrace him just moments earlier. A local Klansman opened fire and killed Evers in his driveway; Myrlie rushed out when she heard the gunshot and found her husband in a growing pool of his own blood. Maxine Smith got to the house within minutes and saw the blood in the driveway. "I still see the blood," she told me. "It was a time when I almost gave up. I was frustrated and scared. I was sure I'd be killed sooner or later, too. But we all had to keep on going."

Local police tried to stop Maxine and other marchers at Medgar's funeral. They would not stop and kept on marching. She held her head up high and was back in the fight. If Medgar could stand up for freedom, how could she not? Evers was ultimately buried with full honors at Arlington National Cemetery.

What sparked the fighting spirit of Maxine Smith? It started long before she was denied admittance to Memphis State University for graduate work in 1957 and responded with what one writer called "thunderous resistance." It was in her system long before she protested the refusal of Gerber's department store in Memphis to permit black people to try on clothes they were considering purchasing; it was boiling in her blood before 1961, when she escorted thirteen black first-graders who subsequently desegregated four all-white public schools. It was alive in her already when she created the "If You're Black, Take It Back" boycott of stores that did not have integrated workforces some fifty years ago.

It predated her principles and courage about the Memphis school system generally—a district of quiet racism and old codes that kept the schools as white as the cotton fields of the basin. She initiated the "Black Mondays" in 1969—school boycotts that inspired a significant number of students, teachers, and administrators to simply stay out of school on those Mondays. The effect of these campaigns—making Smith both the most hated and beloved personage in Memphis—was an eventual restructuring of the school board into representation by wards. This finally opened the way to the election of African Americans to the board—heretofore unthinkable. Smith herself was elected to the school board in 1971 and then served as president in 1991–92. She more or less personally engineered the ascension of the first African American superintendent, W. W. Herenton, in 1978.

But all of these landmark efforts were fueled when she was a child, Maxine Smith said that evening in her living room. It was my wife, Audrey, who leaned forward in her chair and asked: "Maxine, what made you so brave?"

"Brave? I wasn't so brave."

"No, you were, come on." Audrey unaffectedly pressed on. "Maxine, you had a child at home. So many people, mothers, think about the fact they have a child so no matter how important the cause, they say, 'Well, I can't. I can't do this or take this on.' But you did. Were you just born with guts? Were you the kid that her parents said about her, 'She's going to be the death of me, this girl?'" We all shared a good guffaw.

"The truth is," Maxine then responded, "I was inspired when I was nine.

That's when I lost my daddy. Whatever spirit I got, I got from him. And my mama, too, Mudear. That's what we called her, though her name was Georgia. Well back then, wives weren't supposed to work. They were supposed to serve!" Maxine laughed again, that knowing, wise cackle that told us she understood the bitterness underneath the laughter. "But Mudear sure had to take things on when my daddy died." Maxine's mother had been an attendant at John Gaston Hospital in Memphis, and the children grew up listening to the stories of how disgracefully black patients were treated or neglected or simply left to die anonymously and invisibly.

Rev. Nichols then added: "You know, her sister Clementine said their dad was a fireball. And that's where she got that quality from, of being a fireball. Maxine, tell them about what happened when your father was in the hospital. This is when Maxine really realized what she was about inside."

Maxine chortled a bit, her good nature rubbing against another memory that is as astringent as it is illuminating. "Two years before my daddy died, he was in the Veterans Hospital, you see. I went over there, I was only eight or so, with my brother and sister. We knew where his room was and didn't need anybody to tell us where to go or how to be. This white lady, the receptionist, stops us. I said, 'We are going to see Mr. Joseph Atkins.' Well, that lady got all bent out of shape and she says, 'What is this, niggers calling each other Mister?' I didn't know we were supposed to be so respectful like that towards white people, and I didn't care one bit. I knew where my father's room was, so I just kept on walking.

"Let me tell you, that was the ugliest white woman I ever saw. I don't know what she really looked like, but she was just so ugly. Clem and Joe, they said to me, 'Maxine, stop, she's going to get us in trouble.' I said, I don't care if she's going to give us a permit or what, but I just kept on walking. And when we got near his room, I said out loud, 'Mr. Joseph Atkins, please!' And that's really my first memory of being the kind of person I am."

"That's when your fire was born?" I asked.

"Maybe so," said Maxine, sitting back in her chair proudly and with a beaming smile. "Yeah, my daddy worked for the post office, a pretty good job then. But he was worried, his heart was weak, and nobody was thinking about promotions!"

The discussion reverted back to King and his final two days in Memphis. Maxine noted that she hadn't thought of John Henry Ferguson, the young man she collected as he ran, holding his shoes, from the vicinity of the Lorraine Motel just after the shooting of King. "I've got to look him up. I wonder what became of him. Yeah, he was one of 'my bad boys.' He was supposed to be home before dark that night. Hmm."

I noticed the light in her eyes—it was forty-two and a half years later, and Maxine Smith was concerned. She was fretful, just as she had fretted about young people throughout all her decades of social activism and civil disobedience about students, education, safety, fairness, opportunity, and equality. Her face remains smooth and shows no real scars from a lifetime of commitment to and for people that society did not even take the time to ignore. They—the John Henrys, the garbage workers, the janitors, the car wash workers, the black men who always quivered and fled into the urban shadows when they heard police sirens and or just saw the flashing red lights—they were invisible. Maxine hadn't stopped walking, from the hospital ward where she heard her father's dignity excoriated, to the gunplay of Jackson, Mississippi, to the conference halls of the Memphis board of education, to the streets of Memphis on the night when the nation's moral leader was struck down, and on through the subsequent decades of a nation twisting in the smoke of the Vietnam War, the resurgence of social conservatism, and the eventual disintegration of its moral compass in the Persian Gulf and Afghanistan adventures. "Well, we still got a long way to go," she sighed, and laughed, and took her pastor, "Reverend Roz," Audrey, and myself into her arms around the living room table.

We then talked a bit about James Lawson, the deeply focused Memphis preacher who led the strikers of 1968 ("such a difficult time," she said) and remained unwavering in his commitment to nonviolent civil disobedience and to the morning protest marches that he led every single day—from the advent of the wildcat strike to its final settlement in the wake of the assassination. "Jim went to jail for not serving in the army, you know in Korea," she mentioned, recalling the stern, purist nature of his conscience and will. "There was really nobody else like him. He wasn't proud, he wasn't looking for attention. If there was ever a true, nonviolent person, that was Jim. He just did what he had to do."

Having perceived that certain ambivalence from James Lawson toward both the Lorraine Motel and the National Civil Rights Museum during my own discussions with him, I asked Maxine if she knew why that would be the case. "Well, I think that's just Jim. He wasn't even that warm to us at the NAACP. He's just his own man, a complete nonviolence person. I've known him for a long time. He's just his own man, his own thinker. He's not a groupie," she chuckled. "He's not looking for recognition."

Maxine Smith herself is self-effacing about her receiving the Freedom Award from the museum. Others in this circle have included Nelson Mandela, Harry Belafonte, Andrew Young, Oprah Winfrey, Myrlie Evers-Williams, Elie Weisel, Rosa Parks, and Coretta Scott King (only one of two occasions that Mrs. King appeared at the Lorraine Motel site). I mentioned Clinton's comment at that ceremony: "This award is really for Maxine Smith. Maxine should never have had to go through the stuff she went through in order to get this award."

"Well, you know," Maxine responded, "I'm always embarrassed when people do that kind of thing, when they give me that kind of tribute, because I really don't deserve it." This spoken by a woman who sued a school district, helped build a postracial cutting-edge medical center in Memphis, received an honorary doctorate from the university that once barred her from enrollment, and was one of a few African Americans who essentially changed the very complexion of southern society. "People are so good to me, they really are."

"Come on, Maxine, what is the greatness in your life?"

"My greatness? Okay, I tell you what. Because of what I did, somebody else got something good. That's my greatness."

CHAPTER SIX

Saving the Lorraine, Losing the Mantle: Judge D'Army Bailey

O n April 4, 2008, the fortieth anniversary of the assassination of Martin Luther King Jr., a variety of people with assorted agendas appeared at the Lorraine Motel site. Beverly Robertson, the vivacious and highly proficient president and CEO of the National Civil Rights Museum, had her hands full accommodating the press; a swell of visitors; returning civil rights veterans who reminisced, wept, and prayed; and a bevy of Secret Service agents.

Hillary Rodham Clinton, the future secretary of state, converged upon the site: she was in the thick of her still vitriolic race for the Democratic presidential nomination against Barack Obama. In pouring rain, she stood on the concourse beneath Room 306 and reminded everyone of the long-standing connection of her husband, Bill Clinton, and her family to the black community. During the course of the same day, Senator John McCain, the putative nominee of the Republican Party, also showed up and got himself photographed under an umbrella on the balcony outside Room 306—where he made a series of contrite remarks about King, African Americans, and the Martin Luther King national holiday.

He had good reason to, even as both of these potential presidents would have been nowhere else but right there in Memphis at that site on that day. McCain was sorry, he said, that he had consistently voted against the establishment of a Martin Luther King Day, both in Arizona and with respect to the federal holiday that Republican president Ronald Reagan signed into law in 1986. Looking stiff and drenched, McCain said, "I was wrong about that and I apologize."

Billy Kyles did not see McCain offer his remorse, but told me, "Well, I'd be sorry, too, if I were him." An African American visitor who heard McCain dismissed the performance, declaring, "He's got a lot of bones to be here and do that."

During the course of the day, as media people, other politicians, school groups, scholars, and tourists came and went, a broadcast investigative journalist named Amy Goodman set up her microphone and camera operator in the relatively narrow space on the balcony at Room 306. Goodman, slight, fiftyish, and known for being confrontational but extremely literate, is the principal host of a public radio and Internet program called *Democracy Now!* Based in New York, it generally takes a very strident leftist slant on news and events. But today Goodman was in Memphis because she was interested in the story of the Lorraine Motel and its transition to a museum, and she was looking to talk to the museum's founder.

Judge D'Army Bailey, native of Memphis, Yale law graduate, erstwhile city councilman in Berkeley, California, television host and occasional movie actor, a firebrand personality once described by FBI director J. Edgar Hoover as a "subversive" and a "black nationalist militant," is not shy about assuming the title of "founder" of the National Civil Rights Museum. The good-looking, articulate, and generally uncompromising barrister was indeed the driving force behind the museum—only to be ousted from its chair for a "dictatorial" style once the institution was created.

Bailey spoke in subdued tones to Goodman on the motel balcony, recounting in detail the day King was murdered ("on this very spot," Goodman kept repeating, with a certain bit of 11 o'clock news melodrama). Watching the broadcast on video, one can see the mixture of pride, ownership, and hurt that fill Bailey's eyes—he was vital to saving the Lorraine Motel and setting up its future as a national institute, but is now more or less a pariah in the Memphis civil rights community.

He was in New York City on April 4, 1968, he related, and was coincidentally just leaving for Memphis in the morning. He was working with the American Civil Liberties Union (ACLU) on a project to disperse young attorneys throughout the South to help litigate civil rights cases "I had ten law students here in Memphis working with the sanitation workers and their strike," he said.

He left for Grand Central Station in shock. "When I got to Grand Central Station, nobody was speaking to anybody." He returned to Memphis the next day and was part of the sanitation workers' march on April 8 that went on, peacefully, without the martyred leader but now led, stoically and courageously, by Coretta Scott King. Bailey's personal bond to the Lorraine Motel site was created in those days, and he vigorously acted upon it after relocating back in Memphis in 1974.

It was not that he hadn't seen his own heady and dangerous days in civil rights campaigns along the way. After graduating from the segregated Booker T. Washington High School in Memphis in 1959, Bailey entered Southern University in Baton Rouge, Louisiana. His proclivity for conflict not just with white bigots, but with what he perceived as weak or obeisant blacks as well, may have been born at the school: after a notable dash of participation in antisegregation sit-ins, picket marches against Baton Rouge businesses known for discriminatory hiring practices, and a demonstration at the local Greyhound bus depot, Bailey made the mostly black university nervous. When he led a march from the campus into downtown Baton Rouge and subsequently instigated a class boycott, the university expelled him.

Sympathetic and supportive students at Clark University in Worcester, Massachusetts, rallied and raised funds to bring Bailey to that campus. Such scholarships were being offered at several northern, progressively minded schools as co-eds washed cars, ran rummage sales, or simply collected money to "rescue" dislocated young African American scholars from troubled or dangerous academic experiences in the South. D'Army Bailey, powerfully intelligent, irretrievably cynical, has never had a lot of patience with being patronized. In his 2009 book, *The Education of a Black Radical*, he wrote:

> Worcester had rescued me from the big bad land of Cotton, and they were feeling mighty proud of themselves. They were generous, they told themselves. They were liberal; they were progressive; and they were, of course, unprejudiced. Oh, they were thrilled to have me—a real live, Negro activist. They had taken me out of all that turmoil and danger. They had saved me from the incarceration that was life in Dixie and brought me up North, where I could relax, where I could forget all that racial nonsense and concentrate on my lessons. But as they were soon to find out, my career as a civil rights activist was far from over. My eyes and ears were finely tuned to the signs and sounds of bigotry, hypocrisy, and injustice. Obviously, just how they really felt about their new Negro celebrity remained to be seen.

· · · · ·

And then, in an avowal that perhaps portended his coming days of turmoil with and disjunction from the Berkeley city council (from which he was recalled after two years) and then the trustees of the National Civil Rights Museum, Bailey wrote: "I decided to be a person, not a political symbol, and say what I damn well pleased."

Bailey returned to Memphis in 1974 and went into law practice with his brother, Walter Bailey (ironically, the exact same name as the longtime owner of the Lorraine Motel). He has maintained a high profile, as a criminal defense counsel, media personality, unsuccessful mayoral candidate, and circuit court judge. Even his detractors with whom I have spoken readily concede his virtuosity, his charm, and, above all, his indispensable role in the saving of the Lorraine Motel from foreclosure and its emergence as the National Civil Rights Museum.

Bailey invited me to his home—a stately habitat on one of Memphis's many leafy streets—filled with musical recordings, paintings, and treasured relics of his travels and ventures. He is athletic and slim at sixty-nine years of age, with deep eyes that brim with clarity and tenacity. He is, one-on-one, eminently likable and listens well. He has a clear and commanding management of ideas and events and shows no spiritual scars from his many battles and controversies.

One of the first things he told me as we sat down in his living room was that Lucius Burch, so traditionally associated with the defense of Martin Luther King Jr. against the march injunction of April 1968, was "no liberal, not really. Burch was a moderate, maybe, as much a part of the polite white establishment as anybody." He emphasized: "My brother, Walter, defended King long before Burch. Burch just came in at the end and gets all the credit. They want to mythologize Burch, but to me Lucius Burch was just another southern redneck with class. He went hiking and flying and other things. But I'm talking about his fundamental attitudes. We had some disagreements about Rhodesia. He was an apologist for it."

But I had come by to learn about the Lorraine Motel, and he focused keenly on this topic.

"When I returned to Memphis, the motel was a run-down property in a decaying neighborhood on the edge of downtown," he said. "In the six years since Dr. King was assassinated on the motel balcony the local black community, the white business establishment, and the political leadership had done nothing meaningful to rehabilitate the property or to present a dignified tribute to the memory of King. Walter Bailey, the owner, was struggling to keep the doors of the motel open."

Indeed, an account of the situation of the Lorraine Motel and D'Army Bailey entitled "The Crucible" appeared in the *Memphis Commercial Appeal*, written by Preston Lauterbach in April 2008:

Had you gone to Mulberry Street [in the] years after King's death, you would have seen two ramshackle shotgun houses, a raggedy warehouse, an abandoned nightclub, and a lounge around the Lorraine Motel. Aside from the lounge, the only profession functioning near the Lorraine was the world's oldest. Prostitutes rented far more rooms at the rundown motel than travelers, though a few permanent tenants lived there. Weeds pushed through the concrete of the dry swimming pool. Paint flaked from the room doors, a few dangling open from their hinges. Busted beer bottles and broken window glass from the rooms littered the pocked blacktop parking lot.

Lauterbach emphasized that regardless of the site's decrepit and neglected status, there remained a hunger, a curiosity, on the part of sightseers to view a remnant that was effectively disintegrating.

· · · · ·

Visitors still wanted to see the forgotten pivot point of American history. They stood on the broken glass and looked up toward the balcony. The Southern Christian Leadership Conference (SCLC)—the organization King helped found in 1957 and died as president of—installed a plaque and a glass enclosure around the door to Room 306. You could walk upstairs and see the meager shrine inside Room 306. Motel owner Walter Bailey's wife, Lorene, suffered a brain hemorrhage the day of the King shooting and died five days later. Walter displayed her high-heeled shoes and books from her library near the sheet that had been thrown over King after the shooting and the dishes from which he ate a last supper of catfish. A few Ernest Withers photographs of King in Memphis adorned the walls. Visitors could drop a coin or fold a bill to place in a slot outside the display. It seemed fitting, some said, that the place where King's life came to a premature end had become forsaken.

· · · · ·

But it was not at all "fitting," as far as D'Army Bailey was concerned, to see the place simply forsaken. The judge told me about the coincidental, even nomenclatorial nature of his relationship to the Lorraine owner, Walter Bailey. "When I grew up in Memphis in the 1950s, my father Walter L. Bailey was a railroad porter. My mother was initially a barber, and she later became a nurse. We lived a modest existence in south Memphis, in an all-black neighborhood. When I was in high school, perhaps even before, at home I'd occasionally get telephone calls, and they would be bill collectors looking for Walter Bailey. Well, sometimes they were looking for my father, and sometimes they were looking for Walter Bailey, the owner of the Lorraine Motel. And at times, still to this day, there are people in the Memphis community that still think it was my family that owned the Lorraine Motel. I mean, they were both Walter L. Bailey. So I had this sense of identity with the Lorraine Motel and Mr. Bailey just because of that. But I don't recollect that I had actually met Mr. Bailey, or knew him. I don't think I ever even went to the Lorraine, although it was a functioning hotel. We kids would sometimes go to the Lincoln Hotel on Ames Street, for prom and things like that, which was a little bit, a slight degree more fashionable as a black hotel." D'Army suggested that the Lorraine was likely built on a Holiday Inn–type blueprint, replete with a grill and parking lot.

Judge Bailey then recounted the fluke that created a job for his father with the railroad. One day, his father received a call from the railroad seeking Walter Bailey and asking, was Mr. Bailey ready to come to work? D'Army's father hadn't applied for a position but surely needed employment. He hesitated. The white voice on the line inquired impatiently: "'Well, you're Walter Bailey, aren't you? Do you want the job or not?' As it turned out, both Walter Baileys, my dad and the motel owner, eventually worked for the railroad, and they knew each other."

D'Army finally met the motel owner Walter Bailey serendipitously in 1977. "Mr. Bailey was in a Laundromat, and I was in a convenience store next door getting a beer, on the corner of Pauline and Vance. We both exited about the same time, and I saw Mr. Bailey on the sidewalk, and I started talking to him about what's going on down there. If the prostitutes hadn't been providing business, he couldn't have kept the doors open.

"I went down there to the motel after that, and the only kind of shrine they had to King was this encased display on the balcony and in the room where King had been, 306. They got a little income from it because people could leave donations and what not. One wall was lined with books from his wife Lorene's library. He had her shoes in this display case, and then he had the last dishes King used to eat catfish before he died, and he had the sheet that was thrown over Dr. King after the shooting. He had a few Ernest Withers photographs on the wall and some plaques."

I asked, "So it was a memorial for his wife as well as a shrine for Dr. King?"

"That's correct."

At this point I thought to myself: How could such a thing be? How could the memorialization of such a man, an American hero and Nobel laureate, shot in cold blood at the age of thirty-nine, be left to the poor motel owner who happened to be left behind?

Granted, Martin Luther King was not a president or a prime minister. But he did lead and electrify a thoroughly historic and peaceful march of several hundred thousand Americans in Washington, D.C., in August 1963 (the "March for Freedom and Jobs," during which he delivered his immortal "I Have a Dream" address).

The thirty-four-year-old King was introduced at that gathering as "the moral leader of our nation" and was invited by President John F. Kennedy (who had opposed the march for political considerations) to the White House just after the speech. JFK astutely recognized what MLK was and would be.

King joined President Lyndon B. Johnson in the White House time and again following the assassination of President Kennedy on November 22, 1963. He was there for the signings of the Civil Rights Act of 1964 and the Voting Rights Act of 1965—the two most significant pieces of social legislation in American history since Reconstruction. At long last, after Abraham Lincoln's well-meaning but unenforceable Emancipation Proclamation of 1863, after decades of brutish Jim Crow segregation, after a ruthless culture of states' rights–driven exclusion, murder, separation, hyperracism on par with the Nazi regime, and lynching, after southern sheriff fiefdoms that literally intertwined the gory, racialist Ku Klux Klan insolence with "police protection," one man came to personify the change needed to equalize (at least on legislative paperwork) America's two primal bloodlines.

Slave and master, Hebrew and Egyptian, came into the glaring sunlight of America's national story—all through the oratory, mettle, and martyrdom of a modern Moses, and our country at last made a contrite pact with its own "manifest destiny" and supremacist institutions. And this man, for whom postage stamps have been issued, in whose name streets and parks and schools and buildings have been branded, in whose name white housewives, students, priests and rabbis and reverends were brutalized, maimed, or publicly and anonymously snuffed out of existence—this man's legacy would be allowed to crumble and decompose in and around a little motel on Mulberry Street in Memphis, Tennessee? And no one, no state, no federal agency, no national commission would even raise a hand in defense of this heritage?

That is what D'Army Bailey had a chance discussion about on an inglorious Memphis street outside a Laundromat and a convenience mart a few years after Martin Luther King was struck down on the balcony of the Lorraine Motel. It begs the question was D'Army Bailey really a "radical," or was he not acting on a normal impulse?

"Mr. Bailey and I became friends," the judge said. "He really wanted to do something with the place to help memorialize Dr. King. He was working alone, basically, and I knew he really didn't have much of anything and it would be an uphill battle. So he paid me $150 or something like that, and I proceeded to file the paperwork to create a foundation. I incorporated the Lorraine-King Shrine Foundation."

A level of enthusiasm began to spread about Memphis, primarily in the black community. D'Army told me that he approached some white business leaders and invited investment in the project but was more or less turned away.

He also reported resistance from Coretta Scott King and the family. Walter Bailey, the owner, had contacted Mrs. King even before D'Army's involvement, "but they got cross-wired over something. She developed some kind of certain negativity toward the Lorraine early on."

I suggested that perhaps it was just too hard for the widow to acquire any warmth for such a place, given the circumstances. D'Army did not dispute that but also spoke briefly of the Atlanta-centric work of the King family, including, of course, the Martin Luther King Center for Non-Violent Social Change—where MLK and now Coretta are entombed. It was neither the first nor the last time that I got wind of a discernible competitiveness between Memphis and Atlanta over the ownership of the King mantle. One senior member of the National Civil Rights Museum staff sniffed at the Atlanta center outright: "They got nothing there, except the graves! We have all the exhibits and the materials."

In fact, a few years later, when D'Army and his colleagues actually secured the Lorraine Motel in a foreclosure auction, he received a letter from an attorney representing Coretta Scott King. "The letter basically said that we can't use the King name in the project or we'd be sued. So we dropped the name and called it the Lorraine Civil Rights Museum Foundation."

Another person in town who carried a strong interest in preserving the Lorraine Motel was Charles Scruggs, the general manager of the black-owned WDIA radio station (from whence Rev. James Lawson broadcast appeals for calm in the immediate aftermath of the assassination on April 4, 1968). D'Army gives Scruggs a great deal of credit for the advent of the project even though the two eventually came at odds; in fact, Scruggs led the ensuing removal of D'Army Bailey as chairman of the board when the museum opened in 1991.

Chuck ("Mr. Chuck") Scruggs and his staff at the community-minded station were drawn into the narrative when it became clear that the mortgage holder on the tattered Lorraine property, Harry Sauer, was opening foreclosure proceedings. D'Army told me about the occasion when Sauer (evidently not a sentimental man) met with owner Walter Bailey to discuss the loan: "I went with Mr. Bailey to the mortgage holder's house. Sauer had a fashionable house on Yates. I remember sitting with Mr. Bailey and Mr. Sauer in the living room. Mr. Bailey produced a small, brown paper sack, out of which he took the cash and paid it to Mr. Sauer. Now I don't know what kind of records were being kept, but that was how it was at that point in time. I saw that Mr. Bailey was just not going to get any traction, and that's when I tried to get a group of developers to work with me and buy the Lorraine."

D'Army said that if he could have, he would have just bought the place himself.

"Next thing I know, Bailey's being foreclosed." D'Army worked frantically with Scruggs at the radio station. "Charles personally guaranteed a $10,000 bank loan as earnest money." The station manager also claimed to have procured Stevie Wonder for a fund-raising contract though, as D'Army came to realize, Stevie Wonder had not been contacted, and when he was asked, he refused. The concert went on, with the Bar-Kays and some other local acts, but it proved to be a logistical and financial nightmare.

The addition of several other prominent Memphis black personages raised the profile and credibility of the foundation over time, but not a significant amount of dollars. Finally, the foreclosure date was set for December 13, 1982. King had been dead for fourteen and three-quarters years. In his article, "The Crucible," Paul Lauterbach described the drama:

A crowd of curious citizens and TV cameras crowded the Shelby County Courthouse steps on the cold and breezy day of December 13, 1982, to see history sold. The Lorraine foundation had failed to raise the $240,000 to buy the motel's mortgage, making the site of Martin Luther King Jr.'s assassination the featured property at a foreclosure auction.

D'Army Bailey, Scruggs, [and others] represented the Lorraine foundation, with Bailey doing the group's bidding against six others including Harry Sauer, the holder of the Lorraine Motel mortgage. The foundation carried $65,000—$10,000 from Paul Shapiro [of Lucky Hearts Cosmetics] and $55,000 from donations—to the courthouse steps that morning. James Smith, president of the local chapter of the American Federation of State, County and Municipal Employees (AFSCME)—the union of Memphis sanitation workers—delivered to the group a check for $25,000. Other bidders dropped off as the price of history jumped in $5,000 increments. But it became clear to the foundation that their $90,000 would not carry the day, particularly as they looked over at their only remaining competition, Sauer.

As the figure neared the foundation's threshold, financier Jesse H. Turner made it known that Tri-State Bank would loan the foundation $50,000 on a handshake if they could find an underwriter. Willis searched the crowd for friendly faces, and found Paul Shapiro of Lucky Heart to guarantee $25,000. AFSCME's Smith guaranteed the other half, boosting the foundation bidding power to $140,000. Bailey says that he went $4,000 past the foundation's limit, and punctuated his last bid to signal the exhaustion of funds to Sauer. "I bid on up to $144,000 and said, 'And not a penny more.' [Sauer] understood that if they bid again, they were going to own the building."

Sauer went silent, and the gavel dropped.

"It was a glorious feeling," Scruggs recalls.

Bailey concurs, adding, "But it was still a rundown whorehouse. What are we going to do with it?"

Judge D'Army Bailey knew very well what to do with the newly acquired "rundown whorehouse." He closed his eyes for a moment in his living room. He had begun the session by showing me a vintage B. B. King album that he particularly coveted, saying: "I keep looking to have B.B. sign it when I see him next." D'Army knew, back in 1982, that the coalition he had pulled together to save the Lorraine Motel from a foreclosure note consisted mostly of businessmen, politicians, and even speculators who were to be lauded but who all lacked (in his mind) the one thing he had—actual hands-on experience in the civil rights movement. He asserted: "My whole definition of relevance as a black person was from the inner perspective of this movement."

So even the threat of a lawsuit from Coretta Scott King if the King name was used did not deter him. "From my point of view, it was better if we were free of any hold by the family. They had thrown down the gauntlet, so be it. I knew how engaging and captivating and ennobling this movement was. And so, having that perspective, I figured we've got a world-famous site."

D'Army remembered an occasion—before the auction—when he escorted a group of bishops from East Germany to the site. "They went down there, they looked up at the balcony, and they said, 'This is a holy place.' That resonated with me. They weren't telling me anything I didn't already know, but that did accentuate the value of the site. And so, take that site and add to it the spirit of the movement and you have one hell of a facility."

· · · · ·

H as it turned out to be "one hell of a facility"? Has King's blood been consecrated at the Lorraine Motel in the categories of legacy and education? After several years of bitter board haranguing and stillborn fund-raising efforts; of D'Army Bailey inviting moneyed folks (such as white philanthropist J. W. "Pitt" Hyde, who eventually helped depose Bailey) onto the board; of gaining the help of Tennessee state legislators, particularly the esteemed African American lawmaker A. W. Willis; of endless discussions and negotiations with contractors and exhibit builders; and the key hiring of Smithsonian architect Ben Lawless, the museum bumped along to its dedication on July 4, 1991.

After raising nearly $10 million, and with the widespread accusation among the trustees that D'Army had manipulated most of the planning and even imposed the dedication date and the seating arrangements and the inscriptions on the dedicatory plaque—history has risen above the infighting. Despite the self-admitted "filibustering" of D'Army at early meetings in order to ram his agenda through, and his repeated public remonstrations that the museum has sold out to "corporate interests," the museum has emerged as the destination point for millions of tourists and pilgrims since its opening.

One visitor from Philadelphia who stood next to me at the glass outside the restored Room 306, looking in at the coffee cups, the ashtrays, the unmade bed left behind by King and Ralph Abernathy, wiped his eyes and said to me: "This is absolutely the most moving moment I have ever experienced in my life as an American. It's a sacred place, like Mt. Rushmore but with souls." We embraced, no longer strangers in the national family.

Rev. Billy Kyles, omnipresent on the grounds, engaging eager and attentive crowds that form around him to hear The Witness's story, walked with the Dalai Lama on the balcony during the latter's receiving the museum's 2009 Freedom Award. "He just took my hand," Kyles told me. "He just took my hand, and we stood there in silence for several moments. Finally he spoke and said, 'I can feel Dr. King's spirit.' Then we walked back inside. I shall never forget this."

Julie Silver, a renowned religious folk singer from Los Angeles, had visited the forlorn Lorraine during its deterioration period but then returned in 2008. She told me: "I stood there when it was an embarrassment, an eye-sore, in August of 1988. We arrived and the hotel was in complete disrepair, with more homeless squatters than you can imagine. Twenty years later, I got to see how Memphis turned that place into this incredible Civil Rights Museum and will never forget either experience."

The Lorraine Motel is now designated as a "historic site" by the Tennessee Historical Commission. There are other civil rights halls in the United States, including the formidable Birmingham Civil Rights Institute in Alabama adjacent to the historic Kelly Ingram Park—which borders the bitterly famous Sixteenth Street Baptist Church that was bombed in 1963, taking the lives of four little black girls. There is the newer International Civil Rights Museum and Center in Greensboro, North Carolina, which showcases the sit-in struggles at places like Woolworth's and so many lunch-counter sites where the back of American apartheid was broken by courageous youngsters who often were physically brutalized while sitting in for a hamburger and a cup of coffee. Cincinnati now boasts its riverside National Underground Museum and Freedom Center. But the Lorraine edifice is the original, the place made sacred by the blood of the foremost martyr. The director of the Martin Luther King, Jr. Institute for Research and Education, Clayborne Carson, of Stanford University, said to me that the National Civil Rights Museum in Memphis is "preeminent."

"It is, without any question, a national shrine," I was told in 2010 by Otis Sanford, a veteran and celebrated African American editor and columnist for the *Memphis Commercial Appeal.* We sat in his office at the newspaper's edifice on Union Avenue. Sanford, fifty-seven, a large man with many southern annals to his credit, was born in nearby Como, Mississippi. "We were very poor, and I attended segregated schools till the ninth grade." It was evident that Sanford, though congenial and thoughtful, had seen and experienced much that was painful in his lifetime—just because of the color of his skin. He would have had every reason to be cynical about Memphis and its famed, if improbable, National Civil Rights Museum.

"No, the people who were thrown together to make it happen didn't get along, especially D'Army and Pitt Hyde. But somehow they all gave in to the vision that the place just could not be left to disarray. It was a question of the will of the people. It was the scene of such tragedy, maybe that's what made them all determined to rise above it. But the museum is transformational, informational, and educational. I think it possibly surpasses the MLK Center in Atlanta as a center for the study of the whole civil rights story. Everybody eventually got involved, the mayor at the time, Pitt with the financial under-pinnings through his Auto Zone, and other corporations as well. Don't forget about the major role of FedEx. When they came to Memphis, it made a huge impact. The company really does pride itself on diversity and inclusiveness so it also has become a natural patron of the museum."

Then Sanford reflected for a moment and said, "You know, it's really a teaching tool. Something like that—for Memphis—would have been un-imaginable a generation ago." Sanford related a story about his own daughter, Mari-Elizabeth, now grown up, but who first visited the museum "when she was three or four years old."

Mari-Elizabeth actually had a bad experience there. "She was traumatized," Sanford said. "She saw all the pictures and graphics about burnings, lynchings, police beating up on black people. She got really scared that people would do those kinds of things to her mom and dad. Of course, she knows better now, but it was a learning experience. Memphis is so different now than it was in 1968. The kids just do not know from the kind of racism and the voiceless feeling we had. Mari-Elizabeth's closest friend is a Mexican American, and they don't even know the difference. I mean, there is still racial friction. And I've heard the stuff, like people saying to my face that I got to where I am because of affirmative action rather than because of what I do. But it's better now."

Otis Sanford's thoughts drifted back to the evening of April 4, 1968. He and his father were watching Walter Cronkite on the *CBS Evening News* on their old black-and-white Zenith television set. "Dr. Martin Luther King has been shot in Memphis." Otis grabbed hold of his transistor radio and tuned in, naturally, to WDIA; the Lorraine Motel was only fifty miles from the Sanford home. "I was stunned and a bit scared. . . . It's a good thing that they built that museum."

In the end, it seems that the museum was built because of, and in spite of, the discordant Judge D'Army Bailey. As Paul Lauterbach stated it in "The Crucible": "Perhaps, as Bailey asserts, the museum required a bullish, dominant leader to see it to completion. That job done, though, the museum board sought change."

Efforts to unseat D'Army were in full swing within the first year of the museum's opening. Charles Scruggs, the famed WDIA announcer who had been part of the project and the dream to save the Lorraine Motel from the beginning, openly admits to these backroom machinations: "I led the effort to get Bailey off the board," Scruggs explains. "I was chairman of the bylaws committee. Man, they tried to keep the bylaws committee from functioning. What we did was set term limits. I knew that I was out when I agreed to the term limits, but I couldn't think of another way to do it. I crashed the plane with D'Army and me in it. I wasn't piloting it alone, the board was there with me, and there were other people who could've been hurt."

The ever lively and highly influential Maxine Smith made no bones about her intentions when it came to replacing D'Army at the helm. She privately negotiated with Benjamin Hooks, the former head of the NAACP, also Memphis-based, to come in and succeed Bailey.

D'Army describes the sequence in these words: "By the end of 1991, an alliance of whites on the board and some blacks forced new board elections. On the day of the election, Dr. Benjamin Hooks, who had been on the board for ten years but had never been to a meeting, told me, when asked about plans for my ouster, that he knew nothing about any plans to vote me out as president. But the events at the board meeting told a different story. One member presented a letter from Dr. Hooks stating his willingness to accept the position as president if I were ousted in the new election. That being said, Hooks was elected board president in a nine-to-six vote."

D'Army Bailey walked out of the meeting. The Lorraine Motel was left with one broken door. He rarely walks through it but nonetheless walks with his head erect and his eyes open.

CHAPTER SEVEN

Endowing the Lorraine:
J. R. "Pitt" Hyde

Memphis shook when Benjamin Hooks died, on April 15, 2010. The obituary in the *Washington Post*, while highlighting his extended leadership of the NAACP, also cited his presidency of the National Civil Rights Museum along with his receiving in 2007 the Presidential Medal of Freedom from George W. Bush. Over the years, the fiery preacher-attorney had met frequently with Martin Luther King Jr. at the Lorraine Motel.

CBS News quoted from Hooks's last keynote address to the NAACP, which took place in 1992: "Remember that down in the valley where crime abounds and dope proliferates . . . where babies are having babies, our brothers and sisters are crying to us, 'Is anyone listening? Does anyone care?'"

One prominent white leader, a fellow Memphian, certainly did and does care. J. R. "Pitt" Hyde, a soft-spoken but intensive individual, commerce-savvy, effectual, and philanthropic, has for decades been associated intrinsically with the National Civil Rights Museum—as a matter of choice, priority, and corporate sponsorship. Pitt Hyde was one of the eulogists at the funeral of his old friend Ben Hooks; his was one of the few white faces on the pulpit of the Temple of Deliverance Church of God in Christ. The memorial was presided over by Rev. Billy Kyles, and one of several speakers, besides Pitt Hyde, was Beverly Robertson, the director of the museum.

Pitt Hyde, unobtrusively affluent, partial owner of the Memphis Grizzlies of the National Basketball Association, Auto Zone magnate, owner of Pittco Holdings, scion of a family food business, bespectacled, bearer of quiet suits and a low voice, welcomed me into the conference room of the Hyde Family Foundation. We were but minutes from the former Lorraine Motel in what is now the gentrified central Memphis district, crisscrossed by the Memphis trolley system and a selection of trendy restaurants, shops, galleries, Peabody Place, the Auto Zone ballpark, the FedEx Forum arena, and the rib-smoked and jazzy blocks of Beale Street. This is the kind of urban topography that King could have never imagined in his own brief lifetime.

A crystal-clear, oversized window offered an incomparable and sweeping view of the Mississippi River, the basin, and the general green confluence of Tennessee, Mississippi, and Arkansas that mark the wooded, cotton-legacy, steamy coordinates of Memphis.

"Have you seen *The Witness*?" asked Hyde. He was referring to the documentary focused on Billy Kyles, which had recently garnered an Emmy Award nomination after a previous Academy Award nomination. Ironically, I had just come from spending time with The Witness himself, the effusive Rev. Kyles, at the museum. We chuckled about that, both enjoying our affection and respect for the pastor who so personifies the site. But Hyde was asking because he wanted me to know that his daughter Margaret Hyde, a Los Angeles–based photographer and author, was the executive producer of the piece.

"Oh yes, she grew up around the museum and has always loved it, and this is the kind of thing she does. She's so fond of Rev. Kyles, and she said to me that she wanted to do this. So I said, okay, draw up a budget, and we'll make it happen." *The Witness*, running on monitors in between photographic exhibits of slavery, three-dimensional mock-ups of burned-out Greyhound buses and Memphis sanitation trucks, re-created jail cells, and faux podiums from the 1963 March on Washington, is seen and heard ubiquitously in many corners of the museum all day long. It remains a kind of cinematic transcript for the key element of the museum's story—that, in fact, this institution is entrenched and unique because it is built on the very spot of its historical apex, the Lorraine Motel.

Pitt Hyde talks about the events narrated, taught, and portrayed at the National Civil Rights Museum with ease and an informed familiarity. It is his sanctuary, and he has underwritten it with a natural sense of caring heed. Replete with his gravelly yet pleasant voice that does not hide his southern roots, he is so without any guile or disguise (he certainly requires neither because he is fantastically successful and prosperous) that one realizes that this slight, unassuming man, wearing an open-collar shirt and blazer in his conference room, being watched carefully and fawned upon by his genuinely admiring and loyal foundation director, Theresa Sloyan, is exactly what he is purported to be: a decent man who said no to the cultural tradition of his forebears and actually views African Americans as people and their leaders as our national heroes.

He speaks directly about the black colleagues in this enterprise whom he admires (for example, Maxine Smith) and the ones whom he dislikes (D'Army Bailey, specifically, as we shall see). About Maxine, he told me, "Oh, she's so great," he practically gushed—

"She is my hero," interjected Theresa Sloyan, momentarily stopping her meticulous note-taking as we all chatted.

"She's been a close friend since '68," Hyde continued.

"Oh, very close," Sloyan emphasized.

Hyde continued: "It's really funny because I, at a young age, took over the family food business, Malone and Hyde. In the late '60s, anytime any group had a problem or a dispute with a company, civil rights group or whatever, what they would do is picket their neighborhood food markets. Inevitably they'd picket our stores. So I got to meet everybody, from the haulers and pickers to the you-name-it. All of a sudden I get this call from Maxine Smith. And the only person she will meet with is me. Of course, in the food business, if all you put out there are these big guys, your business goes to zip, you know. And so my only knowledge of Maxine at that time is what the newspapers are printing, and they've painted her like some kind of bomb-throwing Bolshevik. So in fear and trepidation, I agreed to meet with her. To my surprise, she walks through the door, and here's this charming, lovely, smart woman, and in five minutes we've worked out what the issues were. And we've been good friends ever since, working on so many projects in the community, the Civil Rights Museum being one of them."

Hyde spoke about "Vasco and Maxine" and "Ben and Francis"—meaning Ben Hooks, whose memory hangs over every discussion about the museum. "Oh, Ben was also one of those classic individuals." It occurred to me that whenever I had conversed with D'Army Bailey about these personalities, he spoke of them in adversarial terms, sometimes bordering on contempt or tinged with ridicule. Bailey may have his reasons. But here was this white veteran of Memphis communal politics and racial tensions, and it was hard to doubt his genuine regard and admiration for these same African Americans. And even if he was polishing his words, he had certainly invested millions of his dollars in their pain.

I asked, "What happened to you that you became such a friend and benefactor to these people and to their causes?"

"Well, my father and grandfather and my aunt were all involved in the community and were great believers in giving back to the community in any form they could. I just kind of grew up with that. Look, I took over this huge business at the early age of twenty-six, so I was in the thick of things from the get-go. It was a kind of baptism by fire. All along, from the food business and then I started Auto Zone, we figured that Memphis was large enough to have all these kinds of problems and issues, but yet it was on a scale that we could get our arms around it."

There was obviously a discernible profit margin that drove the Hyde family to their fluency with poorer people, particularly black people, when one was peddling tomatoes, bread, cereal, over-the-counter remedies, and then automobile parts for a lifetime enterprise (although Pittco Holdings, Inc. has been involved with everything from major property investments to hotels to biopharmaceuticals and biotech research). But Pitt Hyde, for whom everyone in Memphis that I have spoken to has nothing but commendation, seems to be at complete peace with himself and the choices he has made. Time and again, I had been urged to "talk with Pitt Hyde" or had heard the refrain that "without Pitt Hyde, there just would never have been a civil rights museum."

"We could have been running around all over the country, but we decided to focus on Memphis," he said, referring to himself and his wife, Barbara—who is equally active in the Hyde Family Foundation. "We believe that the sweat equity is far more important than the capital. And in the last fifteen years, we really focused on trying to positively influence public policy as well as to support worthwhile things in the community. Now this is really tough because you've got to be very tenacious and take a long-term view on it. We worked on K–12 education for these fifteen years, but the first ten it was like banging your head on the wall. We had a goal, through grants and projects, of trying to create an environment in Memphis that would attract the knowledge workers of the future."

Hyde retired ten years earlier. He does not come across as a man looking for leisure time. Theresa Sloyan chimed in that "he likes the tough projects."

"Was the museum a tough project?"

"Oh yes," he chuckled, but it was evident that the transformation of the former Lorraine Motel into the museum was not a light matter and that it had tried the patience of even the amiable Pitt Hyde.

A. W. Willis, Chuck Scruggs, Jesse Turner, and D'Army Bailey—all African Americans. These were the people that Pitt Hyde cited as the four principals in the saving of the Lorraine Motel property and its eventual transformation into the National Civil Rights Museum. Scruggs was "the WDIA radio personality who raised money." Willis, a towering litigant and politician, moved to Memphis from Birmingham, Alabama, in 1953 and created the city's first integrated law firm; he defended James Meredith and, along with Maxine Smith, helped to desegregate the Memphis city schools. He was the first African American elected to the Tennessee state assembly since Reconstruction; today the A. W. Willis, Jr. Bridge connects the city of Memphis to Mud Island.

Jesse Turner was a major civil rights champion, NAACP national kingpin, and former president of Tri-State Bank in Memphis. He had a public park named for him across from where Elvis Presley Boulevard becomes Bellevue Boulevard—another indication of social progress in the Bluff City. Turner was the first black chairman of the Shelby County Board of Commissioners, where he rubbed shoulders with Dr. Vasco Smith, the late husband of Maxine.

I might have known that D'Army Bailey was somewhat controversial when I first spoke to the wife of Chuck Scruggs on the telephone. When I asked Imogene Scruggs about him (given the historical partnership that is undeniable involving Bailey and her husband), she muttered, "Don't even mention his name."

Pitt Hyde started out more diplomatically. "D'Army Bailey came to me seeking some money for the project. Well, I thought, okay, this is a great opportunity to take a tragic site and turn it into something positive for the city and the country. They asked me to come on the board, and we were the first private money to come into it. They got the state, and they got the city into it." And then Hyde noted: "It was really A. W. Willis who got me involved."

Hyde took a few pauses. He said that the project "sort of ran out of money." It was his way of describing the immediate pattern of bickering and cross-purpose maneuvering that characterized the early days of the process. Over the years, and to this day, Hyde and his foundation have repeatedly made generous gifts to pull the museum out of deficits and trouble—though it historically operates responsibly and with fiduciary standards. Moreover, the many other corporate sponsorships, including FedEx, ExxonMobil, Ford, Nike, Target, International Paper, AT&T, and others (which D'Army Bailey has publicly derided as "part of the pattern of corporate financial control of our civil rights institutions and heritage"), have done nothing if but keep the doors of this national educational shrine open to the public. In general, it has not been easy to get African American history into the general curriculum; it usually has required a prior spilling of blood and a later dripping of guilt.

· · · · ·

Wﾞhen black people live and die, it's the same as for white people, only more so.

After President John F. Kennedy was assassinated in Dealey Plaza, Dallas, on November 22, 1963, Air Force One carried his body and his widow and his devastated staff, under pronounced military security guard, back to Washington, D.C. That was altogether appropriate, of course, and the solemn decorum of it helped to mollify a shocked nation.

After Martin Luther King Jr. was gunned down at the Lorraine Motel, it really was not immediately clear how the business of returning his remains to Atlanta and his funeral would be handled. Though he was a public symbol, he was a private citizen for the most part shunned (and often jailed) by city and state authorities. Coretta Scott King was boarding a commercial airliner at Atlanta's airport for Memphis after hearing from Jesse Jackson at the Lorraine Motel just after the shooting; she literally turned around and returned home after being informed at the airport that her husband had already expired. She did arrive in Memphis early the next morning to retrieve her husband's body.

In fact, Governor Nelson Rockefeller of New York arranged for a charter plane to collect King's coffin and return it and the immediate staff to Atlanta. Even at this stratum of grief and exigency, black people were left to their own wits or to the kindness of angels. So the call from Rockefeller was described by Ralph Abernathy in his memoir as "not only a gracious gesture, but it solved a practical problem for us and made it possible for the family and close friends to accompany the body."

In 1963, when the combined service honor guard that escorted the caisson of JFK practiced endlessly, day and night, for the long processions in Washington and Arlington, they were on government time and had the use of regal military mounts and stallions, shining wagons and regalia.

The planners of MLK's funeral were left to their own wits even as they were committed to convey the martyred preacher's commitment to the poor. They decided to have his simple casket carried on a cart drawn by two mules from Atlanta's Ebenezer Baptist Church to the subsequent liturgy at Morehouse College. These were not provided by a stable or by the state of Georgia. Ralph Abernathy and SCLC senior staffer Hosea Williams had to spend time searching out the red-clayed countryside looking for two mules that would work in tandem. They persuaded a rancher to lend them his mules for the funeral procession of Martin Luther King. According to Abernathy's memoir, they simply appropriated the cart from a remote farm, hoping the proprietor (whom they could not locate) would forgive them, given the cause. Abernathy actually fretted that the owner of the pinched cart might recognize it during the nationally televised funeral and greet them at the cemetery "with an officer and a warrant."

In his own lifetime, King often spoke of the need for racial cooperation. "Like life," he said, "racial understanding is not something that we find but something that we must create. And so the ability of Negroes and whites to work together, to understand each other, will not be found readymade; it must be created by the fact of contact." King disowned the concept of black separatism as being as evil and destructive as white separatism, though he betrayed little patience for polite white liberals who constantly asked African Americans to "wait."

When Pitt Hyde was still young, he rubbed shoulders with and sold boxed cereals and aspirin tablets to black mothers and fathers, erstwhile sharecroppers trying to make it in a city that was perhaps a shade or two less racist than Savannah, Georgia, or Biloxi, Mississippi. His perspective has been "created by the fact of contact." When D'Army Bailey came calling about the crumbling Lorraine Motel (because the black community really lacked the resources to do something and too often went at one another when they tried), Pitt did not see colors or corporations or that many complexities. He saw need and opportunity.

"Over the first ten years, we gave or raised pretty much all the private money. We set up the foundation as a nonprofit so that we could appeal to outside money." Hyde spoke about his first specific gift to the museum—the *Movement to Overcome* sculpture, which greets the visitor upon arrival into the lobby. It is an expansive piece of work, filling up and dwarfing the entranceway. The figures represented are linked together as men, women, and children with no indication of color, race, or ethnicity. They simply represent humankind and a universal cry for engagement against global injustice. When you gaze at the large hunk long enough, you also suddenly realize that you are looking at a sculpted design of the map of the United States.

"Well, I can remember in the early days, at those board meetings, there was all this infighting going on. We sometimes wouldn't get past the reading of the minutes because D'Army would get into arguments with some of the other African American members of the board, and they would be battling back and forth for two hours! And the whole time I'd be sitting there thinking, okay Lord, this is going to be my ultimate redemption."

"Thank goodness you stayed the course," announced Theresa Sloyan.

"It did take all of my willpower. I could just see the potential of this place, and I could see that somehow, someway, we had to take it to the level it deserved. We just couldn't forget it."

Ironically, other African American community leaders in Memphis told me that Pitt Hyde emerged as the mediator among the rancorous black members of the original board of the National Civil Rights Museum—even as they fought over turf, power, control, and recognition. Billy Kyles described D'Army Bailey's leadership and style repeatedly as "un–Martin King." I heard stories of intrigue concerning last-minute altering of the listings of names that appeared on dedication plaques, of board members being denied access to the dais at key occasions, of D'Army basically using the museum as his personal platform.

I found it interesting that it was hard for anyone to definitively recall who the keynote speaker was at the dedication ceremonies for the museum of July 4, 1991. Some thought it was Julian Bond; Bond himself originally told me that he was, then reported to me that no, he spoke at the Memphis Chamber of Commerce that day. (About that, D'Army Bailey told me, "Bond spoke at the Rotary Club, and I arranged it.") Others in Memphis seem to recall that

Jesse Jackson was the keynote speaker; he was certainly there and always makes a large impression. Perhaps here again Rev. Kyles put it best when I asked him about this matter: "I think that D'Army pretty much made himself the key speaker that day."

· · · · ·

Other than admitting that D'Army Bailey was "confrontational," Pitt Hyde would not elaborate about the unraveling of the museum board under Bailey—not to mention the latter's brooding resentment of the Hyde and other corporate money that ultimately extended the life of the museum. The record shows that Maxine Smith (who is hardly shy about this) and others recruited Benjamin Hooks to the board presidency and that Bailey was procedurally thrown out in 1991. As previously stated, few argue that D'Army had not been crucial to the birth of the museum, but fewer would assert that he wasn't ultimately detrimental in style and affect to its survival.

Pitt Hyde, jovial about the approaching twentieth anniversary of the museum in 2011 and thrilled with museum president and director Beverly Robertson, whom he personally recruited, is abundantly proud of the annual Freedom Awards. "We were the original funders."

Hyde crisply articulated that the concept of the museum was to house the history of the civil rights movement up to the time of the King assassination, "but we needed something to honor the people that are carrying the torch forward." The point was made that King's ideas have impacted other global freedom ideologies—thus the list of Freedom Award honorees has included the likes of Nelson Mandela, Archbishop Desmond Tutu, and the Dalai Lama.

Hyde recounted the story—a radiant one—that Billy Kyles had shared about His Holiness, the Dalai Lama, reaching for Kyles's hand on the Lorraine balcony and silently taking in Martin Luther King's spirit for several unforgettable moments. But I had heard enough (and was sincerely convinced) about great people, fine character, important civics, and, by implication, the redemptive power of money when applied from good places in the heart.

I wanted to know about why this was all so important for Memphis, especially since Hyde had been emphasizing all along his choice to concentrate his philanthropic commitment to the city and to the site of King's murder.

"Well, you know," he said, "I think that the building of the museum and the Freedom Awards, which have brought all these people here from all over the world, have helped to build bridges. The interesting thing about Memphis is that we got such a black eye from this when actually we were a fairly progressive city, so the city—you see, it was not so much benevolence but for so long, under Boss Crump, when he ran the city, he wanted to control the state politics, so in order to do that, he allowed African Americans to vote because he wanted to control that vote, so he trained that leadership and allowed that leadership to take hold. So like anything, you know, once you open that door, now you have to start doing things for that group. So we were one of the earlier cities to start the desegregation process and all that. And it really paid off when this thing with King happened. Memphis was really the only city in the country of any size that didn't have riots and such and that was mainly because the quality of our leadership like Maxine and Vasco and Jesse Turner and Ben Hooks is really what kept calm in the city. They took a very active role."

I thought that Hyde, at that moment, was offering a bit of a rose-colored view of Memphis history and that Rev. James Lawson, had he been in the room with us, would have cleared his throat in disagreement and some protestation. Others in both the white and black communities give Lawson and Hooks, for that matter, a great deal of the credit for keeping Memphis relatively calm during the harsh night of curfew and martial law that followed King's murder at the Lorraine Motel as the two pastors roamed the city's poorest and blackest districts (with police passes) pleading for restraint and nonviolence in the name of the martyred civil rights leader. Moreover, when I asked Hyde if he had participated in John T. Fisher's Memphis Cares endeavor in the immediate aftermath of the tragedy, he conceded that he had certainly been aware of it, but that he "was up to my ears in running the business at the time."

In fairness, Pitt Hyde had not come completely into his own in the late 1960s; he recalled dating one of Lucius Burch's daughters as a young man and already being an admirer of Burch ("a Hemingway-type character and a total individual with many interests"). Clearly, something of Burch's spirit and credo influenced him, along with the egalitarian values of his well-to-do family. "You know, Burch always flew his own plane, and he had three crashes!" he laughed. He described his own youthful trepidation as he boarded one of Burch's rickety crafts, overloaded with equipment and gear and diving tanks, "and he never did any maintenance or anything, and we'd load this thing up and the tail would be sitting on the runway and we'd be sweating whether we were going to clear the Memphis-Arkansas Bridge. Then we'd go diving in these remote areas, a hundred and ten feet deep, it was like going down a mineshaft. There were all these fish, sharks, everything. I'm thinking, I'm twenty years old, and I don't want to die while he goes out in a blaze of glory."

Hyde then praised Lucius and the Burch law firm for effectively bringing down the Edward Hull "Boss" Crump political machine, which maintained an airtight grip on Memphis society for much of the first half of the twentieth century and manipulated the black population in what can best be described as a symbiotic relationship. There was irony here, given the previous implication that Crump's reign as mayor, treasurer, and police commissioner had created a progressive atmosphere for blacks, but most Memphians do actually defer to this paradox.

"We've worked with the Burch people on so many different projects over the years," said Hyde.

"They have such a social conscience," added Theresa Sloyan, looking up from her notepad, projecting an astonishing and undeniable bearing of loyalty, skill, and protectiveness.

For some reason, any moment of white people sitting around congratulating ourselves makes me feel a little bit prickly, and I admit to this predilection, and here I was sitting as the guest of one of the most genuinely hospitable, beneficent, sweetest white men I have ever met, who could just as easily have spent that afternoon looking over his ledger of loges at his Auto Zone ballpark. Instead, I was incongruously picking up on some of the D'Army Bailey–style resentment that almost drove Pitt Hyde out of those painful early meetings of the museum board, and then we wouldn't even have a Lorraine Motel facade left standing and a Room 306 balcony or even a sacred bloodstain to move one's heart and tinge one's soul and educate one more redneck and remind one more illiterate that something once happened in a steamy southern city that was a lot more important than cotton, ribs, or money.

CHAPTER EIGHT

The Lorraine Photographer: Ernest C. Withers

n his book *Willie Mays: The Life, the Legend*, James Hirsch writes about the 1948 World Series of the Negro Leagues. For years, when Negro Leagues teams came to Memphis to play the Memphis Red Sox, the visitors generally stayed at the Lorraine Motel—including Willie Mays, who had a brief tenure with the Chattanooga Choo-Choos.

But in 1948 the Birmingham Black Barons, featuring the future New York and San Francisco Giants superstar and "Say Hey Kid," competed against the Homestead Grays in the Negro Leagues World Series. A young, traveling photographer from Memphis named Ernest C. Withers, with a keen eye for African American poignancy and relevancy, and an uncanny ability to be present at the right time with the right people, took photographs of the players, the chalk lines, the sun kissing the meadowlike fields, the sweat-stained rosin bags, the lukewarm water coolers, the wooden bats, and the worn, cloth, dirt-crusted caps. In stunning black-and-white imagery, with which he also ultimately captured the savagery of segregated bathrooms and train stations, the ignominy of grade school apartheid, the rawness of sharecropper hunger, the fatigue and finally the funereal repose of Martin Luther King Jr., Ernest Withers became known as the "Civil Rights Photographer of the United States."

Hirsch notes: The 1948 baseball season "produced one of the most famous photographs in Negro League history. The picture, by Ernest Withers, features the Black Barons in their brick clubhouse after they won the league championship. The jubilant players, many with their shirts off, smiling, cramped in a corner beneath an exposed light bulb and flimsy hangars, a gritty, victorious image of camaraderie, unity, and love. But in the back row, hidden by arms and shoulders, there is a smooth ebony face without a smile, only wonderment and innocence, a boy among men."

Ernie Withers had discovered Willie Mays in the clubhouse, just as he would reveal Martin Luther King Jr. at the Lorraine Motel, studying a newspaper in bed in 1966, and present him at rest in his glass-covered coffin at the Ebenezer Baptist Church in Atlanta on April 9, 1968.

Many years later, Withers spoke with the public radio station at Arkansas State University. Starting out with a Brownie camera, he became internationally heralded for essentially birthing the Civil Rights Museum via his clear and haunting photographs of the Emmett Till murder trial in Mississippi in 1955. (Till, only fourteen years old, visiting the Delta region from Chicago, had been pitilessly beaten, lacerated, mutilated, and shot to death by local whites for allegedly flirting with a local white woman.) Withers documented the 1955 Montgomery bus boycott, the 1956 integration of Little Rock High School, the funeral of slain civil rights leader Medgar Evers, the 1966 March Against Fear from Memphis to Jackson, the Memphis sanitation workers' strike, and, of course, the assassination and funeral of Martin Luther King Jr. He moved freely and easily among King and Ralph Abernathy and their closest aides as they met, ate, argued, planned, and kidded with each other in and around the Lorraine Motel.

Withers, who died in 2007 and was not guilty of bashfulness, spoke about his career experiences, beginning with his start as a military photographer in the South Pacific during World War II:

> In a segregated army, the white kids out on the island of Si Pan where we had no business merchants had a desire for pictures to send home, and I just started a rotating business of taking pictures of the soldiers. So I came out and decided between my brother and I that I should open up a photography studio in my neighborhood. We got the GI Bill of Rights and we bought a building. The career developed in the black newspapers and the transition and growth of American civil liberties and civil rights. I was asked to work and was trained as a news photographer by the people that ran the *Tri-State Defender*, Nat D. Williams, L. Alex Wilson and a number of men who were in the black publication at that time.
>
> Black newspapers across the country, the *Chicago Defender*, the *Pittsburgh Courier*, the *New York Amsterdam News*, the *Philadelphia Tribune*, the *Cleveland Call Post*, the *Kansas City Call Post*—none of these newspapers received wire service of events that involved black people. So the *Defender* had myself linked with L. Alex Wilson, who was a great news editor and writer, and so I was his companion and went into the areas of racial trouble. You know, starting with Mack Parker having been beat down in the jail, the Emmett Till trial, the missing civil rights workers, voter registration, and a number of lynchings that occurred. The black publications at that time dealt mainly with the rights of people. The *Chicago Defender* was the "defender" of African American or black rights. And anytime there was comprehensive or violent type criminal acts against Negroes in Mississippi, Arkansas, Alabama, Tennessee, I was summoned.
>
> "Pictures tell the story" has been my slogan as a photographer for years. I mean, I was in Montgomery when the Supreme Court decision came to Montgomery in 1956 [the decision that ruled against segregation in public transportation, thereby ending victoriously the Montgomery bus boycott]. Martin Luther King rode the first bus, and the *New York Times* and national and international publications used the picture I took because I was the

only photographer on the bus when Martin Luther King rode the bus. He was with [Ralph Abernathy] and Dr. Smiley and the other members of the National Black Church Council. Mr. Wilson woke me up at four o'clock in the morning, "Come on, boy." We went down and got on the first bus that came out of the Montgomery bus station and rode throughout Montgomery. And another hour, hour and a half later Martin Luther King and the delegation came to make the maiden ride, but we had been riding the bus for an hour and forty-five minutes before they arrived to make the maiden ride.

I spoke with two of Ernest Withers's sons, Andrew Rome and Joshua "Billy," in Memphis in 2010. Billy, the elder, lives in California but retains long memories of "a sweet period" in the late 1950s and 1960s when King and many other prominent black celebrities lodged exclusively at the Lorraine, and their father and his crew (including his three sons) intermingled with visitors such as B. B. King, Ray Charles, Aretha Franklin, and Ike and Tina Turner; they photographed, chronicled, hung out, and ate with them. "It was a beautiful place," said Billy. "The owner, Walter Bailey, was very happy, and he loved it when Dr. King was around. It was a relaxed time. King was so personable, he laughed a lot. You'd never know he was the same person that you'd see a few hours later preaching so mighty from a pulpit. Around the Lorraine, he'd be telling jokes, he was just himself. It was a beautiful time."

Andrew (usually called "Rome") has maintained the Withers studios and gallery in Memphis and interacts frequently with the National Civil Rights Museum. The family is deeply rooted in the city; Ernest was once even a Memphis police officer.

If the point of this book is to discover how a handful of people managed to save a motel from destruction and how it then became a heritage house, one might wonder what the place meant to the folks who once lived and worked in and around it. About this, the sons of Ernest Withers are outspoken and sentimental.

Andrew had a close relationship with the owner of the Lorraine, Walter Bailey, and was a young employee of Bailey's. "We'd come in there and eat.

It was one of the best restaurants in the city." By "the city," Andrew, though still in his fifties in 2010, was referring to the segregated city of Memphis and to the Lorraine Grill (so favored as well by MLK) as accessible exclusively to African Americans. "Yeah, we'd come by every other weekend—we'd often take food out. Everything was good till '68, when I was thirteen. Then the rioting broke out, '68, '69, '71, '72. But I was always there at the Lorraine on Saturdays. Saturdays was my workday. Dad was taking pictures of all the people staying there. Then we'd go around Beale Street for more pictures. But the whole weekend, we'd be going with him to football or basketball games, and other events, musical, blues concerts, whatever. It was kind of a lovefest. I'd work around the Lorraine, cleaning up, taking out the garbage, washing ashtrays, and my payday would be a hot dog and a Coke and some kind of John Wayne movie at the theater." Andrew, a serious photographic artist in his own right, was describing a thoroughly happy period of his childhood.

Andrew then did a bit of good chronology for me. He asked about on which of the "three periods of the Lorraine" I was focused—the "before," the "absentee period," or the "after"? It struck me that he was laying down the exact configuration of this history—the prosperity and élan prior to the murder of King; the grimness and dubiety and decay that followed April 4, 1968; the tenuous yet ultimately successful revivification of the motel into the museum by 1991. This is how the Withers family divides the three layers of their lives, contiguously with the three phases of the once and future Lorraine Motel.

While we are approximately the same age, I study the history, but Andrew and his family lived it. I admire King; Andrew took away his plate of catfish bones and handed him a clean ashtray. I gaze at a photograph of King resting at an angle, albeit in an open shirt, studying the *Memphis Press-Scimitar* across his bed at the Lorraine Motel in 1966; Andrew and Billy Withers adjusted the light in the room while their father snapped the shot. These are the denizens of the cotton buds and boll weevil culture, the residents of the sweltering, segregated, southern civilization that I read about as a kid in Cincinnati, but they experienced just 400 miles away as boys in Memphis. So Andrew's inquiry was clarion and trenchant.

I responded that the three periods for me were, essentially, the gathering Memphis sanitation workers' strike in the spring of 1968, which drew King to Memphis three times; the period of some two decades following the assassination, during which owner Walter Bailey had a very arduous time maintaining the motel, keeping unsavory folks away, making the mortgage, and keeping it from decay and foreclosure; and, finally, its transition into the museum.

The Withers brothers and I spoke for a few moments, their tones now heavier, about the sadness that hung over the once jovial owner Walter Bailey in the aftermath of losing both King and, more personally, his own wife, Lorene. They recalled the elegiac alteration by Bailey of Rooms 306 and 307 into a shrine that contained not only some of King's effects and memorabilia but also an exhibit of Lorene Bailey's shoes. This was effectively the original civil rights museum, and the shrine was extensively photographed by Ernest Withers; his young sons would gather up the occasional coin or dollar donations left behind by visitors and turn the funds over to Bailey to help run the declining and neglected and gloomy place.

Billy Withers, who had reveled in the "before period" performing odd jobs and courtesies and working as a serious photographer for the myriad celebrities who frequented the Lorraine, spoke about the "in-between period," which he defined more or less as 1970 to 1978.

"Mr. Bailey was really having a hard time. He was trying so hard to do something with it, to save it. There was a series of people who came through with plans, but nobody did anything. At one point the city wanted to tear it down. They said it had become a transient, prostitution center type of thing. They had declared it as being unhealthy, and also the lights were about to go out. Actually, we had to raise the money. I think it was a Friday. The lights went out, and they were going to destroy it that Monday. I called my former wife and tried to get the money to get the lights back on. I mean, the demolition was scheduled."

As Billy shared this account, I recalled D'Army Bailey's version of this flashpoint with the Lorraine's electricity and his assertion that it was *he* who got the lights restored.

"Well, we got her paycheck," Billy continued (referring to his former wife), "and we saved the whole deal."

Andrew asked his brother, "Do you recall how much it was?"

"I think it was about $160, $170, maybe more. Anyway, I got her check, and we saved the lights."

I said: "Man, you saved more than the lights that weekend. You saved the Lorraine Motel!"

"Well, Mr. Bailey had a lot of pressure on him. To try and keep it open, I'll put it that way. He was so torn between trying to memorialize the place and keep it running, and he had to keep up the clientele that he had at the time. Because by now, this was after integration, you know, so everybody could start going to other hotels."

Billy's fondest memories seem focused on and around 1964—"the era of all the stars, as we call them." The greater world was welcoming the Beatles and the so-called British Invasion that included the Dave Clark Five and other bands. But Memphis, which had already spawned Elvis Presley, was regularly receiving the likes of gospel giant Sam Cooke, Sarah Vaughn, Aretha Franklin, Ray Charles, and Louis Armstrong. The Withers boys routinely rubbed shoulders with—and sometimes even shined the shoes of—high-flying Harlem Globetrotters and the illustrious musicians of Beale Street. Their home away from home was the Lorraine Motel.

"It was a beautiful place," was Billy Withers's refrain. Yet the brothers were not starstruck. "Do you remember how good the food was, Billy?" asked Andrew.

"Oh yeah, I couldn't wait to get out of school and get down there to eat!" Billy responded. I asked if it was true that King and Abernathy preferred the catfish. "Yeah, they did, but I liked the chicken smothered in rice, myself."

"And what was nice too," Andrew wanted to mention, "was the air conditioning. Very modern amenities, not like the fans you found in other places."

"It was a classy place," sighed Billy. "It was always exciting to me because I was young."

It seemed, as one contemplated these two weathered, ruggedly handsome photographers, sons of an icon, that the world itself was once young. There they were, assisting their champion father, that most stealthy and ubiquitous photographer and witness and raconteur of the civil rights chronicle, wiping Elvis sweat and hair cream off of their father's lens, stealing a glimpse of Isaac Hayes and his legendary Cadillac at Stax Records on McLemore Avenue, rolling over in adolescent mirth as King mimicked Cleveland's patriarchal Rev. Otis Moss with wicked accuracy, or catching their breath as their father described King's autopsy (which he had also wiggled himself into): "They put his brains back into his head."

Ernest Withers, in whose veins ran the blood of a newshound, did not frequent the Lorraine Motel because he sought necessarily to be physically close to Martin Luther King, nor did he hang around Ebbets Field simply because he wanted to win the favor of the Brooklyn Dodgers' Jackie Robinson—the Major Leagues' first African American player. "Dad went after the news," his sons emphasized to me. Granted, "the news" for Withers, scrambling across the country in his wood-paneled station wagon, his name printed across the driver's door, was news about black people. It was about fourteen-year-old Emmett Till being exterminated in Mississippi; about policemen who were actually Klansmen who callously executed three civil rights workers in the same state in 1964; about the architecture of segregated toilets and bus stations and park benches in Alabama; about the lynching of teenagers in Georgia; about the I AM A MAN! solidarity of sanitation workers in Memphis. No other person in America has left behind anything resembling the body of photographic work (some five million individual shots) that chronicles the civil rights movement like Withers and his sons and small staff.

When I asked the sons about what their father personally thought regarding MLK, their response was a respectful, "Well, he really was just another person to Dad. He was interested in what was happening, in the history. That's why he was around the Lorraine so much. That's where Dr. King was when he was in Memphis."

· · · · ·

On September 12, 2010, the *Memphis Commercial Appeal* published a major story that would also appear in media outlets throughout the world. Written by reporter Marc Perrusquia, it was headlined: "Photographer Ernest Withers Doubled as FBI Informant to Spy on Civil Rights Movement." It was the lead item on the major television networks that night and the source of extended analysis on cable and Internet sources. It broke hearts and created a marked level of consternation and wrath.

Such stories about possible informants among key civil rights figures have surfaced or have been floated, planted, and sometimes controverted before—particularly in association with King and with respect to his terrible fate at the Lorraine Motel in 1968. It is also an indisputable fact (referenced earlier in this book) that the FBI under J. Edgar Hoover had what can only be described as an irrepressible antipathy toward King, though no government conspiracy has ever been proven or validated in the matter of his murder. (Earl Caldwell, an African American journalist and the only reporter staying at the Lorraine at the time, witnessed the assassination from outside his room, 241. He was on assignment with the *New York Times*. He told me in 2010 that he still believed he saw gunfire from the parking lot level, much closer to the balcony, and that a clump of bushes that were there "mysteriously disappeared" by the next morning. No such assertions have ever been confirmed.)

What is known is that some people were coerced to give information, that others were paid for it, that some had grudges against King, and that some were sick with envy. I have already noted his many adversaries in Memphis—such as the so-called Invaders coalition that violently disrupted his last march on March 28, 1968, thereby humiliating and disgracing him as the national apostle of nonviolent social protest.

Few leaders in the civil rights community, though the assertions gave them a start, would permit the allegations to affect the Ernest C. Withers legacy. A notable exception was the always stern James Lawson, who said, "If he did these things, then he was not one of us."

But Maxine Smith, who knew Withers well and watched him deftly interact in sometimes dangerous situations and record the history, was adamant. Over the phone, she told me: "You can't remove the pictures. Ernie was there, before, during, and after everything. You've got to put things in their time frame. It was a different world then. I saw him get hurt, and get hurt badly. Ernie was not just an onlooker. He operated the way he had to operate. What he gave to us stands."

Billy Kyles shared similar sentiments with me. "I had a great deal of friendship and respect for Ernie. Everyone called me 'Reverend,' but I did not mind that he called me 'Billy.' Because it was Ernie and there was no one else like him. He was in all the meetings, and we gave him access to everything. He knew we were doing civil rights, not plotting to throw down the government. What was he going to expose? Our meetings were open to anybody. He knew what was good, what was not good. He risked his life many times. He was mauled to the point of his life down in Mississippi when he was trying to cover the Goodman-Schwerner trial. You know, they had one line for white journalists and one for black. But they still went after him. He got beat up in Little Rock when he was covering the school integration story."

Then Billy Kyles spoke about the autopsy of Martin Luther King, a subject that had also been broached with me by Ernie Withers's sons. "You know, I didn't go to the funeral home after the shooting. I just couldn't. I stayed around the motel. First off, Ernie instinctively came down to the Lorraine and took some photographs. But I saw him when he took a jar and scooped some of Martin's blood into it. It was sacred for him. You know, he could have sold it for an incredible amount of money but he didn't ever. Then he did go over to the funeral home to see the autopsy. He told us how gruesome it was. At one point, he picked up a piece of skull and put it back on Martin's head. He had his cameras. He could have taken pictures there and made millions. But he did not. That was the kind of man he was."

I asked for a perspective from Otis Sanford, the longtime managing editor of the *Commercial Appeal* and effectively the senior African American columnist in the region. Sanford responded: "For students and other serious observers of the civil rights era, it will be extremely difficult for them to ignore the fact that Ernest Withers, while heroically chronicling the movement, also betrayed it by passing secrets and other information on to the very agency that was out to discredit it. And he was doing it for cash. But I am also convinced that no one will ever deny that Mr. Withers did outstanding work and was a man of bravery. His photographs will remain embedded in our memory forever. But Withers the man was someone who had many forgivable flaws. And do I believe he will be remembered that way."

They are so many of them now gone, the civil rights giants of Memphis and elsewhere, who once walked, danced, sang, slept, made love, and feasted at the Lorraine Motel. As noted, one of them was Ben Hooks, the preacher, judge, NAACP chief, and chair of the National Civil Rights Museum who died in 2010. Hooks was a lifelong friend of Ernie Withers. Hooks put it simply in 2007, when Withers closed his own eyes at last and the cameras of twentieth-century black history were also shut down. Ben Hooks said, "He had a burning desire to shoot pictures."

What would we be and what would we know without the pictures?

PART THREE

THE REBIRTH

CHAPTER NINE

It's a Magical Place: Julian Bond

W hile the United States celebrated its 215th anniversary of independence on July 4, 1991, a ceremonial took place at the site of the former Lorraine Motel, 450 Mulberry Street, in Memphis. The hibiscus trees were basking in the heat and humidity, displaying glossy green leaves that proudly framed their strident pink, red, and purple blooms. The azaleas receded even as the creeks, the rivers, and the wetlands steamed in submission.

After years, even decades, of partisan wrangling, in-community posturing, hard fund-raising, much second-guessing, but with a pervasive sense that the Lorraine Motel could not be relegated to the blood and dust of history, a hearty, if sometimes cantankerous coalition of citizens, clergy, philanthropists, politicians, historians, zealots, skeptics—of all races and creeds—had pulled it off: on that day, the Lorraine Motel, which had been foreclosed in 1982, was being dedicated and reborn as the National Civil Rights Museum.

Judge D'Army Bailey, in his capacity as chairman of the museum's board, presided over the event. Bailey, always a subject of discussion, once interacted with Malcolm X and remains a high-profile legal eagle to some but "an ambulance chaser" to others. Nonetheless, he had held the cacophonic trustees together since spearheading the successful auctioning of the Lorraine mortgage in 1982. He consigned all the board members, including civil rights icons such as Benjamin Hooks, Billy Kyles, and Maxine Smith, to seats in the audience and limited the places and speakers on the dais. "Heck, I even allowed Jesse Jackson only two minutes," he told me.

Another featured speaker in Memphis would be Julian Bond, the handsome, eloquent, scholarly yet activist cofounder of the Student Nonviolent Coordinating Committee (SNCC), longtime Georgia state representative, future chairman of the NAACP, and guest host of NBC's *Saturday Night Live*. Bond had just completed his role as narrator for the *Eyes on the Prize* PBS documentary, both parts one and two, a year earlier. As part of the citywide observances, Bond keynoted at the Memphis Chamber of Commerce and joined other dignitaries at the museum's launch.

"It's an iconic place," he told me from his home in Washington, D.C., where he is a professor of history and the civil rights movement at American University as well as the University of Virginia. "It was a great honor for me."

But even the erudite Bond may not have known all the details of the near-miraculous salvaging of the Lorraine Motel. It began as the whites-only Windsor Hotel in the mid-1920s, ostensibly serving clients as a brothel, then was renamed the Marquette Hotel as the Second World War ended in 1945. It was then offered for sale.

As we know, the site was purchased by an African American entrepreneur named Walter Bailey. The neighborhood had deteriorated and was no longer favored by whites. Bailey and his wife, Lorene, had attempted several businesses, including, at one point, managing a turkey farm. The acquisition of a special lodge for black folks, one noted for its comfort, conviviality, and unpretentiousness, was a dream come true for the Baileys. As noted by the historian Michael K. Honey, Walter and Loree (her familiar name) sought a "homey atmosphere enjoyed by black entertainers such as B. B. King, the Mighty Clouds of Joy, and others." Walter Bailey was quoted as saying: "In your business, you gotta be one big family. I don't think we'll make it in the world if we don't get together and make it one big family."

Walter renamed the place the Lorraine, after his wife and a song titled "Sweet Lorraine." At the time of purchase the Lorraine included sixteen rooms, a café later frequented by King and his cronies, and living quarters for the Baileys. "King was their pride and joy," reports Honey. Little did Walter know that his beloved Lorene would die of shock and cerebral hemorrhage that struck her within moments of the shot that killed King on April 4, 1968. She lingered for a few days and expired at St. Joseph's Hospital—where the preacher was pronounced dead. Lorene, just fifty-two years old, passed away on the day of King's funeral in Atlanta, April 9.

The assassination destroyed the motel's viability as a business. Walter kept his additional job as a clerk at the nearby Holiday Inn and eventually remarried. His own death, in July 1988, occurred just three years prior to the dedication day of the National Civil Rights Museum. Walter Bailey's passing was noted in a *New York Times* obituary; he was seventy-three.

The future of the Lorraine Motel grew increasingly uncertain after King's assassination. Bailey tried to operate it, offering only a few rooms, but to no avail. Many of the room keys were stolen; one had to check in via the front desk with each entry. The spot seemed destined for blight and dust.

Some people in Memphis did not care what happened to the site. But a cluster of prominent local citizens created the Martin Luther King Jr. Memorial Foundation for the sole purpose of saving the motel. Even his detractors concede that D'Army Bailey was the catalyst with many key connections and a powerful, clamorous personality. "If you want to know all the facts," Julian Bond told me, "talk to D'Army."

The foundation raised money, solicited donations, took out a loan, and partnered with a company called Lucky Hearts Cosmetics and radio station

WDIA to purchase the motel for $144,000 when it went up for auction follow-ing a foreclosure notice. The cosmetics company, which sells skin products to African Americans and is located adjacent to the motel at 390 Mulberry Street, is owned by a Jewish family named Shapiro. Paul Shapiro put up an initial $10,000 "to stop the wrecking ball"; he died in 1993 and left a major bequest to the museum as well.

With the intermittent help of the city of Memphis, Shelby County, and eventually the state legislature of Tennessee, enough funds were procured to formulate, design, and build what would eventually become the National Civil Rights Museum.

The fund-raising efforts were intense, but they actually fell a bit short. The creators of the museum were absolutely determined to launch the site on the landmark July 4, but the museum did not fully open to the public until September of that year. It has since drawn over five million visitors from all over the world.

Bond remembered: Present on the day of the dedication, along with himself and Hollywood luminaries Blair Underwood (*L.A. Law*) and locally born Cybill Shepherd, who had won the "Miss Memphis" pageant in 1966, was the governor of Tennessee, Ned McWherter. McWherter, says Bond, also spoke that day. He was the one who had, as a state representative, garnered the key appropriation in the Tennessee House to actually save the property for official purposes. The governor recalled that on the night King was killed at the Lorraine, he was on a patrol as a National Guardsman, trying to keep the city from completely exploding in violence and rioting.

"There was another southern governor in the crowd," Julian Bond told me. "A fellow named Bill Clinton." Bond laughed to himself. "He hadn't quite announced for the presidency yet, and nobody really knew who he was. He didn't seem to be enjoying that and was jockeying for some attention." Clinton, from Arkansas, would be elected president in November 1992.

"Bill Clinton?" I asked Bond. "Why would Bill Clinton have been there?" I didn't recall D'Army mentioning anything to me about the former president.

"Well, I guess he must have figured that even though it was Independence

Day, and governors do go around attending official things in their state, he was probably better off being seen at this event that eating some barbecue somewhere in Arkansas."

Charles Newman, the attorney who had sat directly across from Martin Luther King and Ralph Abernathy in Room 306 on April 3, 1968, with his boss, Lucius Burch, as they rushed to prepare a court presentation against the injunction preventing King from marching with the sanitation workers on April 8, was also present in the crowd at the 1991 dedication ceremonies. He recalled the articulacy of Julian Bond's address but also remembered the milling about of Bill Clinton.

"I said to my wife, 'there's Bill Clinton,'" Newman told me. "He looked a little lonely and anxious. I noticed he was off to the side, talking to a highway patrolman. My wife said, 'You ought to go over there and say hello to him.' I thought about it but just didn't. Kind of sorry I didn't, given what happened with him so soon after."

· · · · ·

Julian Bond, now a youthful seventy years old, still with a clear baritone voice and distinguished enunciation, a man of letters and declamation, has nonetheless led a life with many contentious and dangerous crossroads. He was first inspired to apply his skills and convictions to the civil rights movement while a student at Morehouse College in 1960. He had been stirred by the lunch-counter and restaurant sit-ins taking place in Nashville and Greensboro. He was a hands-on student and disciple of James Lawson and Martin Luther King Jr.

In March of that year, he and King worked together and initiated a meeting on the Morehouse campus; the first Atlanta sit-in under the aegis of the "Nashville Student Movement" took place in the aftermath. The movement eventually included the perilous Freedom Rides that proved, against ferocious white resistance, that African Americans could ride buses and trains across interstate lines and use public facilities. (The "Nashville Movement" still exists in that city—a community coalition that in 2010 was working on campaigns promoting economic justice for Nashville taxi drivers, car wash employees, and low-wage workers generally.)

Bond, an active swimmer and one-time intern at *Time* magazine, then became a founding member of SNCC and served as its communications director for several years. From 1960 to 1963, as John F. Kennedy was elected president and served his brief term, Bond was highly visible in student protest actions against the segregation of public facilities in Georgia. He also emerged as the first president of the Southern Poverty Law Center, which still battles hate and discrimination as a not-for-profit legal agency.

Julian Bond notices things about people—even the ways that they dress, talk, and interact. He once reminisced about Ella Baker, the fiery, independent, and brilliant so-called Godmother of SNCC who, in a remarkable lifetime, helped to foster the NAACP, the Southern Christian Leadership Conference, SNCC, and the Mississippi Freedom Democratic Party. Julian sensed that the younger Baker did not especially trust the more senior leaders of the movement—including even Martin Luther King (although King was only in his thirties in the 1960s!). Bond recalled "her warning against entanglements with adults . . . just to keep our movement pure. That we had started it, we had carried it forward, and we could carry it on by ourselves."

Bond, with his mellifluous choice of words, described Ella Baker, who was known for her organizational abilities and her outspoken advocacy of women in the male-dominated African American organizations that she helped steward. "Very regal," said Bond. "Always had a business suit that she'd wear—a long skirt, and it had a long jacket. She was sort of matronly in a not-dominating way. Like 'Don't do that, be careful, don't do that.' In a very nice way, but very much your mom." While many of the male leaders dismissed Baker because she was neither a minister nor a man, Bond recognized an inherent greatness in her that has always influenced him. Baker was memorialized with a U.S. postage stamp in 2009.

Bond also intuited about the emotional undercurrents that existed between and among some of the giants of the civil rights movement. When both James Lawson and Martin Luther King spoke to protégés at one of early gatherings, "We had this real sense of friendly rivalry between Lawson and King. Not any personal animosity between them, but Lawson was like the bad younger brother pushing King to do more, to be more militant, to extend nonviolence—just to do more."

The work that both Lawson and King did culminated in the historic federal civil rights legislation of the mid-1960s, particularly the Voting Rights Act of 1965—all under the tutelage of President Lyndon B. Johnson. The voting bill, which finally enfranchised African Americans in the South, delivered eight blacks, including Julian Bond, to the Georgia House of Representatives in 1965. However, the legislature voted to deny Bond his seat because of deep displeasure with SNCC's (and Bond's) public opposition to the Vietnam War. There was further antipathy because Bond believed that young men should be allowed to resist the military draft that was dispatching so many of them to Vietnam. He also proposed that young people should be excused from conscription if they made a conscience-driven choice instead to work for civil rights in America.

The case wound up being heard by the Supreme Court in 1966, after a U.S. District Court upheld the Georgia assembly's ban. Friends and acolytes gathered around Julian; the situation was not without its spiritual and physical stress for him—he broke into hives, and he did not simply breeze through this crucible. Martin Luther King took up Bond's cause in his speeches, declaring, "We are in a dangerous period when we seek to silence dissent." Bond, who had been King's student in a philosophy class back at Morehouse College, actually put King in a tenuous situation: MLK endorsed the resistance to the draft as a pacifist but conceded that he personally would not be a party to draft-card burnings.

Nonetheless, the Supreme Court settled the matter (and rescued King) with a 9–0 ruling that the Georgia House of Representatives had denied Bond the right to freedom of speech and that he had to be seated. Bond served four terms in the Georgia House and then six terms in the Georgia Senate.

In 1968 Julian Bond came into the national spotlight unwittingly. Just weeks after the murder of King at the Lorraine Motel, the Democratic National

Convention convened in Chicago. Robert F. Kennedy had also fallen to an assassin's bullets; the convention, dogged by nonstop protesting outside its doors and in the streets of Chicago, became an internationally broadcast tempest of anger, grief, disillusionment, and intergenerational contempt. With Bobby Kennedy gone, the delegates nominated Vice President Hubert H. Humphrey for the presidency (he would lose a close election to Richard M. Nixon in November).

Julian Bond was unexpectedly nominated for vice president. A generation before Barack Obama, this was the first time that an African American had ever been so designated by a major political party. "I didn't win," he said humorously on Minnesota Public Radio in a 2008 appearance. But Bond also spoke of the irony of that week in August 1968: he remembered the tear gas and rampant beatings and clubbing of citizens by Chicago police and several thousand National Guardsmen in Grant Park, in Lincoln Park, and in the streets. He himself had marched outdoors with student leaders on Tuesday evening, August 27. "On Wednesday, August 28, I was nominated for vice president." He received 43 percent of the convention votes before he had time to react.

In his memoir, *Walking with the Wind*, the civil rights legend and longtime Georgia congressman John Lewis recalls the moment. "It was a protest, a maneuver. . . . Julian handled it extremely well, very low key, very reasonable, very impressive." Significantly, the two men, once close, became estranged after their bitter electoral battle in 1986 for the seat that Lewis has held since then. Lewis wrote: "[Julian] was a national symbol now, both of the opposition to the war and of the new generation poised to inherit the nation's political mantle, the 'radical chic,' as the magazines were calling it."

Bond was only twenty-eight years old and knew that he could not accept the nomination. The Constitution requires that both the president and vice president be at least thirty-five years of age. He graciously withdrew, but he understands that the symbolic event helped paved the way for the concept of an African American serving at the highest level of government.

· · · · ·

Julian Bond was devastated and incensed when the news came from the balcony of the Lorraine Motel on April 4, 1968. He was 400 miles away, in Atlanta. He declared the next day: "Brotherhood was murdered in Memphis last night. Nonviolence was murdered in Memphis last night. All that is good in America was murdered in Memphis last night."

It is fairly safe to say that, in his sorrow, Bond recalled the more innocent times he shared with King while Bond was his student at Morehouse College. "That's when I knew him most extensively," he told me. "I was one of only eight people in the class. It was a class in philosophy. But I have no memory of what transpired in class because each session wound up becoming an informal discussion about the civil rights movement. What happened in Montgomery, how the bus boycott was set up and how it worked. That's what he loved to talk about."

Bond seemed to relish sharing a yarn with me that has followed him around for decades and—he admitted mischievously—is based on a bit of fiction. "The story goes like this: One day, after our Morehouse class, Dr. King and I were walking across the Morehouse campus, and I said to him, 'How are you doing, Doc?' His friends called him Doc. He said, 'Julian, I'm not doing well. Unemployment is high, segregation seems immovable, racism is everywhere. I feel awful. I have a nightmare.' 'No, Doc,' I said. 'Turn that around. Try "I have a dream."'"

Julian took in a breath. "While I did take the only college class that Martin Luther King ever taught, the story is fiction, and I usually tell it as a joke before my speeches. But then on one occasion, a man introducing me read my biography, and then said, 'Now, the man who taught Dr. King to say, "I have a dream," Julian Bond!'"

Bond paused on the phone, allowing me to take this little fable in. What was not allegory was the unmistakable affection for his teacher—it was palpable over the phone line. The story was as real for Bond as the loss of King remains so grievous more than four decades later.

I asked Bond if he thought King should have gone to Memphis in the spring of 1968. His answer was immediate: "Of course he should have gone! His presence was critical to the situation with those garbage workers. He could never have been dissuaded from going somewhere because of any circumstance. Look, it was dangerous to go anyplace for him."

Perhaps Julian Bond contemplated the reality, the danger that was so endemic to the brief and tumultuous life of Martin Luther King when he first saw the permanent bloodstain on the balcony outside Room 306 of the Lorraine Motel. It brought up complicated and conflicted feelings for the man who once joked with "Doc" after class at Morehouse College. "Frankly," Bond told me, "the first time I was there and saw the bloodstain, I was repulsed. It was terrible, I thought, even ghoulish." The enduring presence of the stain created an ambivalent stalemate for Bond concerning the Lorraine Motel.

"But in time, I changed my mind, and see it very differently now," he continued. "It's appropriate and belongs in that spot. Someone died there, and he didn't die naturally. It occurred to me that the stain is an important part of the shrine. This was an evocative moment for me."

He was enthused and privileged to be part of the dedication of the National Civil Rights Museum on July 4, 1991. "It's so good that it's there. It's so well preserved in this format. They have done such a great job, the way you can literally walk through the site and experience the history and look into Room 306 just as it was. It would have been such a shame if it hadn't been saved and had just gone into urban decay. Now it's an iconic place."

Bond recalled for me taking a tour group sponsored by the University of Virginia through the museum and former motel in 2007. Ironically, they convened with an attorney who had sat with King in Room 306 at the Lorraine Motel the day before the assassination—Charles Newman. Newman recounted the dramatic session for them, when Lucius Burch quickly assessed King and realized that he had to take on the case of the injunction against the sanitation workers' imminent next march. Bond told me, "The fellow was terrific in recounting that meeting. He sat right across from King and Abernathy in the room, and they just talked. Abernathy handed him some ribs, and they ate right there on the beds."

Julian Bond's Memphis tourists were enthralled and deeply moved by the living history of the Lorraine site, he stated. "In fact," he suggested, "I wish the museum would have some kind of booth that would allow people to record their comments and feelings as they walk through. It would be really significant. It's a magical place."

In the exhibition section of the museum that displays the chronicle of SNCC, there is an original typewritten memo to SNCC leadership from 1964. It was typed by Julian Bond and is directed to all prospective SNCC members; it is entitled, tongue-in-cheek, "How to Be a SNCCY."

I mentioned Bond's suggestion of an oral testimonies booth for visitors to Beverly Robertson, the director of the site. She immediately agreed, grabbing a pen and making a note to herself. "Yes, we should have those." The Lorraine Motel remains open.

CHAPTER TEN

filming the Lorraine:
Lillian Benson

illian Benson's father did not want to see Martin Luther King Jr. visit Memphis in the spring of 1968. He thought King should just focus on civil rights and avoid the labor dispute in Tennessee.

Lillian, now an admired television, video, and cinema editor, and the first African American female member of the American Cinema Editors, an honorary editing society, was studying fine arts in college. Among her manifold credits, perhaps her preeminent acclaim is for editing the King episode of *Eyes on the Prize 2,* the multiple award–winning television series. She was only the second in her working-class family from New York City to attend college—following her elder sister. Calvin Benson was happy about that and proud of his daughters. Like many men of his generation who fled the Deep South, he believed that education and faith in God would provide a better life.

Calvin had spent years working as an elevator operator in New York City hotels. He turned the heavy wheel, allowing people to come and go as they required. Open the doors, let people in, press the up and down buttons, and exist invisibly. Especially if you were a black man. It wasn't Richmond, Virginia, or Jackson, Mississippi, or Macon, Georgia. But it was still the veiled, servile world of brown-skinned workers filling out a day of tedious, monotonous toil. Not a lot of fresh air or encouragement or gratitude enlivened the world of the elevator operators who have labored in the cavities of contemporary buildings and skyscrapers. Calvin may have traveled vertically up and down all day long, but his life was horizontally constrained by society's rules of race and its limitations on the movement of black men.

"I'm not sure why my father was so afraid of King going to Memphis," Lillian Benson told me from her office in Los Angeles. "Maybe his feeling about King was just premonitory. Or maybe it was because he was a union man, and the sanitation strikers were taking such a risky stand. My father was a member of the hotel workers' union, but he did not think the black union in Memphis could be successful. And he was worried about Dr. King."

As a child, Lillian did not experience formal segregation growing up in urban New York City, "other than the occasional and painful little reminders that came in certain ways from some white people." But she did see the blight of Jim Crow when the family took the train car to vacation with aunts and uncles and cousins in rural sections of the Carolinas, such as "Colored Only" signs in the railway stations and cafés and "Whites Only" signs over drinking fountains in the downtown department stores.

Lillian's parents' grandparents were bona fide slaves. "I would see the plantations of my ancestors as we drove along the countryside on our way into town," she reminisced, her voice wistful and plaintive. Calvin took in deep breaths as the family rolled along in the countryside. Heavy history must have pulled at him as he held the steering wheel. Said Lillian: "He grew up with his grandmother who had, as the saying goes, 'worked in slavery.' My mother's father was 'still in knee pants at Emancipation.'"

Years later, in a better America (she asserts), she collaborated with the renowned choreographer and director Debbie Allen (*Fame*) on a number of creative television projects with other directors on programs for PBS, Lifetime Television, and other venues. She has edited projects about Native American history, the Great Depression, Motown, the Alvin Ailey American Dance Theater, and the notorious censorship by CBS of the Smothers Brothers. But a deep part of her heart—and inspiration—remains in the Carolina fields and in the cautionary words of her father about the young preacher who would make his final deviation to Memphis, Mason Temple, and the Lorraine Motel.

Like many others, Calvin Benson had been right to fear Memphis. Two garbagemen crushed to death; sewer and drainage workers driven home by rain without the pay their white counterparts retained; police tear gas; a haughty mayor who absolutely refused to recognize the legitimacy of the sanitation workers' union and told the men to "go back to work because public workers are not permitted to strike." Even the I AM A MAN! placards hoisted defiantly on the workers' shoulders as they marched daily that spring—though they stirred the hearts of working men—made him more anxious about the safety of Rev. King.

Lillian's father likely did not know that King's closest advisers shared his concerns and pleaded with him not to divert to Memphis. Andrew Young was quoted as saying: "The staff was really disturbed that Martin would even consider going to Memphis." Part of the unease was about logistics; the Poor People's Campaign was still gestating and needed concentrated effort and fund-raising, and King was so overextended and exhausted that Young mused bitterly about his mentor's "war on sleep." But the specter of losing King to assassination was always there, and the staff did not really know how to protect him in the already fiery and capricious environment of the so-called Bluff City.

Memphis officials had been receiving threatening messages, telegrams, and even published letters in the local newspapers that put King in potential crosshairs. Threats of intimidation and menacing innuendos originated from sources such as the Ku Klux Klan, the White Citizens Council, and sundry white supremacists and maniacal individuals who derided and excoriated King as the real source of the racial unrest in Memphis and the Delta region.

He was racially eviscerated as "Martin Luther Coon." This current of hate and endangerment was all but matched by the vociferous campaign on the part of J. Edgar Hoover's FBI to discredit, malign, and imperil King. Calvin Benson was as prescient as Lillian suggested to me, as MLK's closest staff was apprehensive.

Lillian Benson, soft in tone though firm in conviction, thinks a lot about the presence of evil in the world. "I see it as ever-present," she told me. "I don't think it is really evident to most people." A life in film editing, often films that deal in the racial anguish of America, has informed her soul deeply in the matter of goodness and malevolence. "It is goodness that requires strength. The goodness in me, I think, has always been in need of growing."

Tapestries of kindness and iniquity commingle in Benson's mind and shape her memories. The shadows fall and recede as she contemplates the vicissitudes of life; she does a great deal of spiritual editing. She vividly recalls April 4, 1968, when the assassination at the Lorraine Motel changed the underpinning and path of her life, and the news came to her like an unwelcome wind from a terrible place.

"I was returning from dinner, at a restaurant near my college campus, with my friend Roberta. Evil came to us. A mutual friend of ours came by and told us, 'Dr. King has been shot.' It was a shattering moment. The world continued to spin, but nothing was ever the same. I mean, people said that, I remember, at 9/11. They said that nothing would ever be the same, and of course that was true. But really, nothing was the same or would ever be the same from the moment we heard that Dr. King was killed."

· · · · ·

Roberta lingered in Lillian's mind as she conveyed the story. "Roberta, my friend, was a Jewish girl, from Westchester. It was so strange because April 4 was her birthday. But then, in 1983, Roberta was murdered." It was a random, senseless act of evil, Lillian now stated, drawing her breath short on the phone. "I remember the whole fateful circle. When Dr. King died, it was April 4, Roberta's birthday. And she had just told me two days before, she told me to cry when I had to. She said that it was okay, that it was important to cry."

Thirty years later, on April 4, 1998, in a gathering commemorating the milestone anniversary, Lillian Benson stood in the section of the National Civil Rights Museum that is the remaining facade and interior of the original Lorraine Motel. The balcony is there, the railing, and that section of former rooms that includes Room 306. A wreath is maintained on the doorway of Room 306 that is regularly refreshed. Like so many others before her and since, Lillian peered through museum glass into Room 306, the "King-Abernathy Suite," where MLK had so often slept, eaten, made calls, met with people, and enjoyed a covert cigarette. Benson was, of course, the consummate film editor and artist, but this day she was simply Calvin's daughter and a grieving American.

"I looked into the room," she said, softly, tenderly, "and saw the teacups, the napkins, the bed with the blankets and sheets unmade. It underscored for me the frailty of life, that you can be here, and then you can be so suddenly gone."

Thoughts of Roberta swirled up in Lillian's head, and she reflected elegiacally about her friend's admonition to weep. April 4, the day King was shot here. April 4, the day Roberta was born. And then she recalled the days just before Roberta's murder: "We had just spoken with each other. I told her, okay, I'll see you on Sunday. She was dead on Friday." Good and evil struggle with one another in the shadows and through the glass of Room 306.

$$\cdots\cdots$$

M emphis evoked a powerful response in Lillian Benson as she visited the city in 1998. "I may have had more of a reaction to the environment in Memphis than some of the others who came. It was my first time there." Benson had seen the celluloid images of the Lorraine, Mason Temple, the police in riot gear, while editing *Eyes on the Prize.* She had heard many accounts and descriptions from people such as Andrew Young, Ralph Abernathy, Marian Wright Edelman, and Julian Bond, who narrated the distinguished series. But now, at last, she was there, on the thirtieth anniversary of the assassination, and she moved through the actual locales of the saga she had seen in stock footage. "It was holy ground," she made clear.

I could hear her delight as she told me, "I stayed at the Peabody Hotel—it was a matter of principle, since it had been denied to blacks for so long."

"And you saw the ducks marching through the lobby?" I teased her.

"I saw the ducks marching through the lobby," she agreed, triumphantly.

But the genteel hotel is not her defining memory. Lillian reminisced: "It was eerie walking down the same streets past the Clayborne Temple just like the strikers did in the footage I edited in the King episode of *Eyes 2*." Clayborne had been the origin or destination site of several actions during that spring of 1968—it was to where some 1,500 maced, burned, beaten, nauseous, terrified people retreated, many of whom were led and guided by the injured James Lawson, in the aftermath of the police riot described in chapter 4.

Lillian Benson saw and heard Rev. James Lawson in 2010; the occasion was the screening of director Stanley Nelson's documentary called *Freedom Riders*. Lawson's thick silver crop of hair grew out of his head like a beehive of wisdom, and his eyes were still bold and taunting. After the screening, he talked to the filmmakers about the movement, the Freedom Rides, the Memphis campaign—all of which he remains a feisty veteran. "Listening to him," she shared, "I felt like I hadn't really done enough, certainly not at the level of giants like him." A certain inadequacy lined her soul—she thought of her moment at the glass of Room 306 and wondered what she and her contemporaries could possibly do to match or at least parallel the efforts of Lawson and the others who, in the 1960s, from Birmingham to Nashville to Memphis, had endured beatings, tear gas, hunger strikes, and prison to progress the cause. Then someone in the audience asked Lawson, "What should we be doing?"

The mighty pastor paused and reflected, without a trace of affect, superiority, or guile. He looked out and said, simply: "Make movies. That's what you do."

"It was so energizing and wonderful," Benson rejoiced with me. "He really meant it, and it made such sense. They did what they had to do in their time and in their circumstances, and now we had the means to continue the work through what we happen to have and what we do."

·····

n 1998, during her milestone visit to Memphis, Lillian Benson had joined other film artists at the enormous and historical Mason Temple—site of several fuming rallies on the part of the sanitation workers in 1968 as well as MLK's final and prophetic "Mountaintop" screed. "I sat in the same seats that I had seen in so much stock footage," she declared. Her thoughts swiftly went to imagining the actual scene, the moment, the drama and divination of the night of April 3, 1968, after King was called to come over to Mason Temple from his brooding perch in Room 306 of the Lorraine Motel.

The Reverend James E. Smith of Memphis, a minister who unwaveringly supported and suffered with the sanitation workers' strike, later became the paid director of their first established union. He declared about April 3, 1968, the night of the "Mountaintop" speech: "It was an overcoming spirit in Mason Temple that night. We knew that we were going to win. Dr. Abernathy spoke well. But we were waiting for Dr. King. And because he was in town there was an overcoming mood, an overcoming spirit in that place. . . . There was something about Dr. King. A man who could walk with kings, but he was just as simple when he spoke that all of us understood him. Never met a man like that before."

So Lillian Benson, sitting in those very seats, felt "the overcoming spirit." That night, thirty years later, Everett Goodwin, known as "Bill Clinton's preacher," filled the hall with his own mellifluous tones of praise and tribute to a real epoch. Though many of the civil rights greats were there, including former Lorraine Motel guests Jesse Jackson and Andrew Young, Benson particularly recalls this preacher. "He spoke about Dr. King in biblical terms," she said, "of King the prophet coming to Memphis, who would not see the promised land." Once again, the old walls of the tabernacle, walls that had heard a suffering prophet in 1968 preach the fear of death out of himself, heard a more modern voice lifted by the inspiration of King's scriptural wounds and visions.

· · · · ·

yes on the Prize, a fourteen-part documentary series chronicling the civil rights movement, is enshrined in the Museum of Broadcast Communications in Chicago. It won some twenty-three awards, including two Emmys, and was televised by the Public Broadcasting Service. The first six programs, *Eyes on the Prize: America's Civil Rights Years (1954–1965)*, were aired in January and February 1987. The eight-part sequel, edited by Lillian Benson, *Eyes on the Prize 2: America at the Racial Crossroads (1965–1985)*, was broadcast in 1990.

The effect on the national community of this comprehensive, carefully written photojournalism, with its stark footage of beatings, police hosing of black children, spiteful white mobs, bombed churches and burning buses, lynching incidents, institutionalized segregation in American cities, and the wrongful imprisonment of leaders from Rosa Parks to James Lawson to Martin Luther King Jr., resonated across cultural lines. Donald W. Murphy, the one-time deputy national director of the National Park Service and now CEO of the National Underground Railroad Museum and Freedom Center in Cincinnati, told me:

> *Eyes on the Prize* captured a transcendent moment in history when a segment of humanity rose up to keep a promise that it made with itself. The promise was to eventually overcome our collective bad angel and realize liberty, justice, and equality for a disenfranchised people. The singing of "We Shall Overcome" still rings in my ears and reminds me that humanity as a whole has not yet fully kept the promise. If the human race is to survive, we must all be overcomers. That is the message of the program for me.

Steve Hirschberg, a practiced and longtime writer and reporter for National Public Radio (NPR), calls *Eyes on the Prize* "absolutely riveting and the best documentary series I've ever seen. I remember that it began with the trial and execution of Emmett Till, who had the sheer audacity to actually whistle at a beautiful white woman that he saw on the street. Unfortunately for him, he was not in his native Chicago when he did this. He was in Money, Mississippi, and was viciously tortured and murdered. This was really the galvanizing moment of the civil rights movement."

The executive producer of the series was Henry Hampton, who died in 1998 at just fifty-eight years of age. Hampton was a young survivor of polio who participated in the "Bloody Sunday" march across the Edmund Pettus Bridge in Selma in 1965—his idea for *Eyes on the Prize* was born in that historic conflagration. In 1968 he founded Blackside, Inc.—a breakthrough minority-owned production company. The brilliant St. Louis native, who experienced racial bigotry firsthand as a youngster, eventually succumbed to cancer.

Benson remembers that Hampton gathered all the artists together as they began work on *Eyes 2*. Even though the follow-up production would deal with various issues, people, and events, and would tend to focus on smaller narratives and on some unheralded heroes, Hampton started the creative process by asking them to focus on one moment, one day, one incident: "Where you were on April 4, 1968?" Benson closed her eyes, of course, and was back at college, with Roberta, as evil and blood and disbelief thrust at her from the balcony of the Lorraine Motel in Memphis. That place, that blast of evil, remains the locus of the story, for Lillian, for Billy Kyles, for James Lawson, for Charlie Newman at the Burch law firm, for Julian Bond, and for the 200,000 visitors who visit the National Civil Rights Museum and pause underneath the balcony and the wreath every year.

Hampton was able to raise the funds for the original series with relative ease. Corporations and foundations did not have much discomfort underwriting an educational program, well conceived and with excellent production values, that told the stories of Rosa Parks and the Montgomery bus boycott of 1955, the emergence of a very young Martin Luther King Jr., the *Brown v. Board of Education* case that officially outlawed segregation in public education in 1954, the Freedom Rides, and the passage of the 1965 Voting Rights Act.

Hampton was not so fortunate when it came to developing *Eyes 2*. He barely raised the $6 million necessary to pull off the sequel. As media historian Frances K. Gateward has written: "The reticence of both corporate and public granting organizations is attributed to the subject matter of 'Eyes 2,' issues which the United States [had] not yet resolved: the rise of the Black Panther Party, the Nation of Islam, the Black Consciousness Movement, the Vietnam War, busing, and Affirmative Action."

Just as the struggle became more complex for MLK and the movement following the legislative victories of the mid-1960s, and a new brand of leaders, more inclined to violence and separation, began to push him and others to the periphery, so did American anxiety about racism and economic justice became ensnared in fear, anger, resentment, and hostility as King died, the war in Vietnam escalated, the "Silent Majority" appeared, and a new conservatism took hold.

On August 28, 2010, the forty-seventh anniversary of King's "I Have a Dream" speech at the Lincoln Memorial, Fox News commentator Glenn Beck was able to mount a huge and successful "Restoring America's Honor" rally at the same site—heavily peopled and funded by the "Tea Party" movement of the era. Granted, a sprinkling of African Americans, including King's niece (and brother A.D.'s daughter), Alveda King, appeared or spoke at the overwhelmingly white, jingoistic rally that also showcased former Alaska governor Sarah Palin. A counterdemonstration, led by Rev. Al Sharpton, the de facto and controversial civil rights spokesman of the postmodern era, which also featured Martin Luther King III (highlighting the tragic personal divisions that pervaded King's children and descendants), and which decried Beck and the Tea Party's rather cynical co-opting of MLK's mantle, drew far fewer participants.

Henry Hampton would likely have had no chance to fund a documentary about the American human rights saga of the twenty-first century, and there would be little stock footage worth editing. Ironically, the election of the first black president—while it seemed to consecrate King's dream and his blood at the time of the 2008 vote—swiftly set off a palpitation of new racism, xenophobia, and national social angst that paralleled the relentless economic swoon. Martin Luther King III would not talk with me for this book, politely citing "family and personal reasons." One of Henry Hampton's colleagues who worked on the *Eyes* projects told me—on strict condition of anonymity—that

"Henry would have never gotten such a piece through. The atmosphere is so ugly now. Nobody at Ford or any of those companies would give him a dime. They just get bailed out, and it's about the rich getting saved and the poor drowning in Katrina. Who'd fund a documentary like that now?"

Little wonder that Lillian Benson feels the pulse of good and evil in her own heart. Henry Hampton understood what happened at the Lorraine Motel—and at so many other such places across the years of the nation's war with itself. He wrote: "We are aware of the danger in presenting history that may not have fully settled into clear perspective. . . . Our times seem to be ones of retreat from the dearly won gains of earlier generations."

Hampton was gone before the chilling crucible of 9/11 (the stuff of documentaries now, along with endless video projects and television series and movie sagas depicting terrorism, international rage, American self-hate, and looming nuclear Armageddon). All the unyielding cinematic historians who have tried to save America from the jaundice of ignorance have continued to persevere—just as an unlikely group of Memphians and others eventually saved the Lorraine Motel and converted it into a freedom museum.

As Henry Hampton also declared, "While the headlines of racial violence are frightening, nothing is more disturbing than to listen to young men and women who appear to have no sense of what brought us to where we are. How can you enter the debate if you fail to consider what has happened?"

· · · · ·

The relationship of the Lorraine Motel and its environs to the personal journeys of artists such as Lillian Benson is significant. The balcony and the tragedy of Room 306 are depicted in a number of films, including even the biopic *Ali* starring Will Smith as the iconic heavyweight champion. It is a visceral issue for Charles S. "Charlie" Robinson, a veteran stage and movie performer who appeared in the 1978 television miniseries *King* as the real-life Detective Ed Redditt of the Memphis Police Department. The three-installment production, lasting 300 minutes, starred Paul Winfield as Martin Luther King and Cicely Tyson as Coretta Scott King.

Robinson is a muscular, approachable man who appears significantly younger than his sixty-five years. He is best known for his long-running performance as bailiff Mac Robinson in the NBC series *Night Court*. Nonetheless, as he conveyed to me, no role on stage or screen has meant as much to him as his portrayal of Redditt—the investigator who was inexplicably called off from his surveillance of MLK at the Lorraine Motel just prior to the assassination on April 4, 1968.

"When I understood the role and what was actually happening to my character, it hit me really hard," said Robinson, who clearly embraced the role and its historicity. "I felt it, I felt this great guilt and confusion about being called off, all of a sudden when I was supposed to be protecting King at the time." Charlie Robinson began to talk like a true actor, subsuming the character into himself. He vividly recalled looking into a peephole for binoculars created through a newspaper that was taped onto a window and intensely scrutinizing King from a fire station adjacent to the Lorraine Motel.

In fact, Ed Redditt was a Korean War veteran, a one-time track star who grew up on Beale Street. When he became a police officer in Memphis, he discovered that there were regrettable parallels between the way the department treated its black officers and what was happening in all the other fields—including sanitation. His bent was toward working in community relations, but the department assigned him to plainclothes "intelligence" work—Redditt may have been one of the officers appointed to Police Commissioner Frank Holloman's all-black security detail for the protection of MLK. This unit was described to me by Rev. James Lawson, as noted in chapter 4.

Writing in the magazine the *Christian Century* in 2000, author James W. Douglass asserts:

On the afternoon of April 4, a black Memphis Police Department detective, Ed Redditt, was removed from his surveillance post at Fire Station 2. Redditt had been watching King and his party across the street. Redditt testified that MPD Intelligence Officer Eli Arkin came to Fire Station 2 later that afternoon to take him to Central Headquarters. There he was brought to Police and Fire

Director Frank Holloman, a retired FBI agent. During his 25 years in the FBI, Holloman had been head of the Memphis field office (1959–64) as well as J. Edgar Hoover's appointments secretary. Holloman told Redditt that a Secret Service agent had just flown in from Washington with information about a threat on Redditt's life. He ordered him to go home.

"I objected," Redditt said. "Director Holloman told Arkin to take me home." When they arrived at Redditt's house, the car radio announced that King had just been assassinated at the Lorraine Motel. Redditt testified that nothing further was ever said to him by the authorities about the threat on his life.

Two other African American officers were known to have been puzzlingly removed from their posts associated with the Lorraine Motel in the hours just prior to the assassination. Redditt was particularly exercised and suspicious about being recalled; he had personally interacted with King during the preacher's visits, eaten with him, and even lamented the biased practices of the Memphis Police Department with him. The officer had been meticulously logging all the activity around the balcony and Room 306, including the comings and goings of the so-called Invaders, whom King was trying to placate and neutralize in advance of the planned April 8 march.

But now, talking to actor Charlie Robinson, I was almost persuaded that the voice on the other end of the line was actually Detective Ed Redditt. "Abby Mann [director of *King*] told me to watch Dr. King and not to take my eyes off of him. It was so hard for me when they told me to leave my post. I was watching everything right across the way at the Lorraine. After Dr. King was killed, I felt such overwhelming guilt because I had to leave my post. I was supposed to have protected him."

It should be noted that the former detective Ed Redditt played himself in a 1992 television feature called *Who Killed Martin Luther King, Jr.?* Also appearing as himself was The Witness, Rev. Samuel "Billy" Kyles. The Lorraine Motel, now a museum, has continued to be the source of much celluloid creativity—and for actor Charles Robinson, the most important script of his life.

And for Lillian Benson, who gazed through the glass of Room 306 and saw the teacups and the napkins and felt humanity's vulnerability, the Lorraine Motel will always be "a reminder that once we know what is right and good, we have to summon the courage to stand up, regardless of the possible cost. Society today seems to say that the traits that made King great—tolerance, cooperation, charity, equality, and nonviolence—aren't worth much, that they are in fact signs of weakness, not of strength. We don't celebrate these kinds of 'weaknesses.' As Dr. King said, 'Darkness cannot drive out darkness; only light can do that.' In my opinion, we all need to be a little more like 'the light.'"

CHAPTER ELEVEN

Managing the Museum at the Lorraine: Beverly Robertson

"Oh, it was a struggle," said the lively, middle-aged, buoyant mother of three adults who has been the president and executive director of the National Civil Rights Museum since 1997. Beverly Robertson, a clear-eyed Memphis State University graduate and veteran of the Wharton School of Business and the Getty Museum Leadership Institute, does not appear to be a person daunted by any struggle. But the "struggle" she referred to, as we sat together in her busy office at the museum, just several hundred feet from Room 306, was the effort to wrangle control of the museum's original board—and its future—from Judge D'Army Bailey.

She started the discussion as diplomatically as possible. "I really think his heart is in the preservation of this history. But I think sometimes our own personal drives or inclinations can interfere with that. But, again, his heart is in the preservation of it so that other generations can understand it in a different kind of way. And so I hear D'Army's rhetoric, but I really believe that underneath all of it is this desire to take something that was really tragic and turn it into something triumphant."

Earlier that same week in September 2010, D'Army Bailey had posted yet another criticism of the museum on his Facebook page: "It is sad and offensive that the National Civil Rights Museum has further sold our legacy of struggle to the monied and corporate interests of Memphis with the Museum's public support of the November ballot proposal for city-county consolidation. The consolidation proposal maintains two separate and unequal public school systems and should be resoundingly defeated."

This was a serious political issue in Shelby County, and the retired judge's opinions on such matters carry weight and significance. But it was hard for many people to disassociate his views and convictions on education, jurisdiction, and partisan considerations generally from his well-known and bitter personal imbroglio with the National Civil Rights Museum. While most people I spoke to in the museum community qualified their criticisms of Bailey with the perfunctory, up-front, "he's really smart," "he's charming," "no D'Army, no museum" (all of these axiomatic), Bailey never returned the courtesy. To his credit, he never sprinkled saccharin on what he was serving.

So when the conversation with the decidedly professional Beverly Robertson turned early on to her champion and the museum's undisputed chief benefactor, Pitt Hyde, it was not so easy to be ambassadorial.

"I often ask him about those very turbulent early years," she said. "I ask him, why did you stay? White man, investing in this history?"

"And a bunch of black folks screaming at each other," I offered.

"Well, vilifying him. Screaming at each other and vilifying him. That was my issue. The way they treated him. And I asked him, why did you do it? And he said, because I knew that this was something that was really important. It was worth staying for."

Robertson quickly reviewed a more recent disruption within the museum leadership that dragged on for two years where she felt personally attacked—"and this was led by D'Army, and I knew that"—but she swore Pitt Hyde "to stay out of it. This is not your fight. First of all, I don't want it to end up being a black-white struggle. Okay, so the white guy—you say he's taking over, I don't want that. Let him deal with me."

As I listened to the details of television stations being called and then called down, of statements made and detracted or withdrawn, though Robertson was circumspect, I kept hearing Billy Kyles's description of these little wars on the holy ground of the Lorraine site as being so "un–Martin King."

There was ample pain in the voice and narrative of Beverly Robertson as she tried to pit her frustration with these intermittent flare-ups (which, of course, echoed the even greater ruptures of Bailey's initial presidency of the museum board) against her better nature. One wanted to somehow assuage her. So I spoke up: "Look, Beverly, I have to tell you. Speaking as just one devotee of the history, as a white guy from San Diego who loves this place and has been mentored by the legacy of Dr. King, there just isn't much awareness, if there's any at all, about this out there, generally. When I have studied the written and video records of the fortieth anniversary of the assassination and all that happened here at that milestone, you saw a fair amount of D'Army Bailey. There were interviews outside Room 306 with him, and he was always dignified, and in many cases he was the face of the museum and was often referred to as the 'the founder of the National Civil Rights Museum.' But this rancor and this infighting, it's just not part of what came across."

"That's lovely," she said, a bit flatly. And then her enthusiasm returned as we focused a bit on the seminal marker of April 4, 2008. She remembered the extraordinary people, politicians, clerics, and artists who congregated at the site from all over the world—from Rome, Africa, South America, and every corner of the United States. "It was a kind of global convergence," she remarked. "And that's when we realized how much this place means to everybody, to the point that we had to reevaluate its branding. You see, everybody would say to themselves, 'Okay, I know what the Lorraine Motel is.' And we had been calling this place just the 'National Civil Rights Museum.' It occurred to us, when Ann Curry and all the other national anchors came and said, 'This is Ann

Curry reporting from the Lorraine Motel,' we literally rebranded ourselves as the 'National Civil Rights Museum at the Lorraine Motel.'"

The talk turned to the often enigmatic Rev. James Lawson. Robertson expressed the desire to "get Jim Lawson more involved with the museum." So many others had described the sense of aloofness, the kind of taciturn quality coming from Lawson that was more than obviated by his fierce and ardent commitment to justice and dissent and nonviolent protest. "I remember him even when I was a little girl," said Beverly. "He was a Methodist seminarian. Sort of a very spiritual kind of guy. Smart and scholarly. But also very influential because he led out of passion and what was right. He was all about peace. And you know, he never wanted any credit for anything. He was always very self-effacing."

Robertson described Lawson as the "linchpin" of the Memphis sanitation workers and civil rights stories—which history bears out. It was Lawson, much more than Kyles, who specifically prevailed upon MLK to come to Memphis. Robertson said that she wished Lawson would be more availing of the museum's community and programs—she voiced his compelling fittingness for a Freedom Award.

"Well, I think Jim Lawson expects people to come to him, more than the other way around," I offered.

"We *have* gone to him! We have tried many times." Beverly was animated. "I've told Barbara [Andrews, the education director] to go to Nashville and sit down with him if that's what it takes. I'll go to Nashville myself if that's what it takes. People get confused sometimes about who got things done. Lawson, with his quiet demeanor, was moving and shaking here in Memphis. And we are expanding our local Memphis history section here. There might have been loudmouths out there during those days. But he was the one doing the work and getting it done."

"Well, every single day of the strike, he was out there leading the daily march," I felt compelled to point out. "Even the morning after the assassination, after he was up all night keeping the peace in Memphis."

Growing up in Memphis, looking up to the "Black Princes"—the eminent clergy who stood up for African Americans who had little other social or civil recourse—it is no wonder that Beverly Robertson retains vivid memories of the defiant, Gandhian, unbendable Rev. Lawson, pastor of Centenary Methodist Church during the 1960s. And Lawson made it clear to me that he has little patience for the gleaned stardom of, say, a Billy Kyles, or the kind of necessary commercialization that comes with the making of a museum. For him, movements, marches, sit-ins, freedom, hunger strikes, prison sentences, lunch-counter demonstrations—these are liturgical, doctrinal, and sanctified. He stands apart from a lot of fine people who, by necessity or disposition, nonetheless mix ethics with prospects.

So, too, it would seem, with Beverly Robertson. I asked her if, when she was growing up in Memphis, she ever imagined that she would be sitting in such an office, presiding over a museum that houses both the American civil rights story and the death shrine of Martin Luther King.

"No, I could not have imagined that, but I know that growing up in Memphis was a very positive experience for me. My father was a truck driver, and my mother was the kind who stayed home with the kids. My dad was really the smartest person I've ever met in my life, but because he was African American, he didn't get close to anywhere maximizing his intellect or his ability. He would often train people at his company to do his job, and then they'd be promoted above him, and those were often white men. But he harbored no resentment. He was a dominant, domineering sort of a guy, but very soft-spoken. He was just glad to be able to provide for his family."

"What was his name?"

"John Cato. Yes, he was soft-spoken, but when he spoke, you listened. My mom was with us. She went to everything with us, the schools, the PTA meetings, and both of them really instilled in us, when the times were at their worst with segregation that—you know what? You are as good as the next person, you are equal. If you work hard, you can succeed. Don't let anybody destroy your joy or dampen your spirit. So there was this can-do spirit in the family, and we didn't feel poor. I never knew we were poor till much later—I was wearing my sister's hand-me-downs, but everything was all right, and if one of us thought, okay, I think I'm going to become a brain surgeon, then he'd become a brain surgeon.

"I remember one Christmas, I told my dad the only thing, the one thing I wanted was a little bottle of fire-engine red fingernail polish." Beverly's voice rose with a crescendo of remembrance and affection. "So when I woke up on Christmas morning and saw my little bottle of fire-engine red fingernail polish"—Beverly was laughing with pleasure now—"it was just the best. I grew up in a loving, caring environment. If we didn't always have new clothes, our hair was brushed, our faces were scrubbed clean, and anything less than an 'A' from school was unacceptable."

Robertson described the "awesome teachers" she and her classmates had in the segregated Melrose High School ("I was a Golden Wildcat!"), people who were guided by a sense of mission and perhaps even ancestral destiny during the years of the civil rights transformation. "Our teachers were so into us. It didn't matter that we were in inferior buildings, that we got used, marked-up textbooks handed down from the white schools. They were old and tattered and torn. We didn't care! Oh, the life we led then. I had a teacher once—I have to tell you—you had to have seen this woman. She stepped up on her desk one day and started her dancing—"

Suddenly, I was beholding Beverly Robertson standing up at her own desk, scarf flying, hands flinging, eyes blazing, actually singing in what was something of a gospel strain: "*You gotta get up for yourself! Nobody's gonna do your thinkin' for you. You better think for yourself!*"

The president of the National Civil Rights Museum at the Lorraine Motel straightened her outfit out, smiled, and sat down. "How could we not do well? We got that kind of reinforcement every day." Robertson was beaming.

"What was her name? The teacher, I mean?"

"Mrs. Echles! E-c-h-l-e-s. Minnie V. Echles."

. . . . .

I t was funny, it was honey-sweet, it was declarative, it was bold, and it was touching. And then, it was oh-so-troubling. Textbooks for information-hungry, intellectually curious, knowledge-seeking American school kids being garnered via throwaway, tatty, already handled and marked-up tomes that could only be pristine when christened by white students in whites-only public schools? An entire national minority, upon whose back the sectional economy had been built for centuries, all of it in the form of a modern throwback to Egyptian bondage, remaining corralled into separate learning, dining, shopping, and lavatory spaces even after black and white GIs (in segregated units, of course) defeated the fascists at an unspeakable cost from 1941 to 1945? And John Cato, Beverly's father, still had to pass along his skills to white men rather than to utilize his skills among all men in the 1950s? Long after the betrayal of Reconstruction, America retained the barbed wire of visceral racism and contempt for a cross section of ourselves simply because that part of us has black skin?

Why did the African American children in the bowels of Memphis not have home heat when the ice storms of winter howled across the basin and caused their teeth to chatter and their legs to ache and their hearts to pound? The great oaks outside would crack from the concussions of cold while white kids would snuggle next to sweet-smelling fireplaces and under thick down comforters, their bellies content and filled with hot food and peace, from Montgomery to Memphis and back to Atlanta and Tallahassee. Nor did immunities truly exist from this insipid social segregation and apartheid in places like Cleveland, Philadelphia, Boston, or Chicago. King went to Chicago, in fact, in 1966, futilely attempting to liberalize the city's housing laws so that black and Hispanic families could have a chance at a better life. He reported that he had never known such overt racism from housewives and school kids who pelted him with epithets and stones; he conceded that he had never been more afraid.

Why does Otis Sanford, the well-informed, fluent, and recognized columnist and editor at the *Memphis Commercial Appeal*, still get roused about "only making it because of affirmative action" and still have to throw it off? Why does Rev. Marvin McMickle of Cleveland, one of the most brilliant and erudite pastors and scholars in the region, a Ph.D. in divinity and the author of twelve books, always well groomed and distinguished, still have to notice young white mothers snap their purses shut and pull their children close when he happens to walk by?

Why did Benjamin Hooks, a pastor and a judge, the venerated NAACP trailblazer and chairman of the National Civil Rights Museum, who led the Dalai Lama around the museum hand-in-hand, have to struggle with bladder problems all his adult life because he was routinely denied access to public bathrooms a good deal of his life? Which culture actually read the poorly marked textbooks?

No wonder people come to the museum that Beverly Robertson runs with good spirits and a vigilant eye—to sort out their emotions and guilt and confusion about why they and we, all of us, have been effectively duplicitous in what was one of the longest-running crimes against humanity on this planet. Yes, you can go to Dealey Plaza in Dallas, where President Kennedy was gunned down in brilliant sunshine on Friday afternoon, November 22, 1963. You can go there and walk about the well-appointed Sixth Floor Museum in what is the former Texas School Book Depository Building; you can even crouch in the so-called sniper's nest above Houston and Elm streets and speculate about trajectory, science, forensics, and conspiracies.

But when you come to Mulberry and Main in Memphis and you visit the former Lorraine Motel, what you examine mostly is yourself. Yes, you can inspect the infamous window and bathtub across the way in the "annex"—the one-time seedy rooming house of Bessie Brewer, from where the assassin is alleged to have fired the single shot that snuffed out the life of Martin Luther King Jr. You can eyeball a duplicate of his getaway 1966 Mustang in which he stalked King, from Los Angeles to Selma to Memphis (where a bit of tragic serendipity found him staring out the bathroom window at his cosmically vulnerable victim that Thursday evening).

But what you do accomplish mostly is what one visitor summarized for so many: "It is a very emotional experience. I was physically and mentally exhausted after this experience. The site of the Lorraine Motel is forever more sacred ground where once again the world learns you may kill the Dreamer but you only make the Dream stronger." Beverly Robertson may talk about maintaining top-notch dress codes for her staff, she may be in a constant tussle with time management, she may fret about the multimillion dollar development campaign in full swing to coincide with the museum's twentieth anniversary in 2011, and she certainly grieves personally as, one by one, the aging legends of the civil rights movement pass on. But her ultimate goal for this facility, this hybrid of motel and museum, of blood and biography, is exactly what that visitor recorded in the guestbook. "Dr. King," the guest wrote, "was change for God by man."

· · · · ·

Beverly Robertson, now a key steward of Memphis and national history, retains vivid memories of the years prior to and following the assassination of Martin Luther King Jr., including the desperate working conditions of the city's sanitation workers (virtually all black) and the hostile indifference of the local government. "What really led to this," Robertson told me, "was that we had a mayor who felt that the dues check-off that the workers were asking for was illegal. He was untenable in his position."

Robertson was speaking of Henry Loeb, upon whom his neighbor John T. Fisher could not even prevail to show some compassion or less rigidity during the crisis of 1968 that brought MLK to Memphis.

She remembered thinking as a teenager at the time, living in that city, "How cold and heartless can you be? These guys are being forced to work when others are getting days off. They make much less money. They have families to feed, how could you be so cruel? They were toting these big nasty buckets on their heads, maggots everywhere, go home and maggots in your shoes. The conditions were just so terrible for the African American workers. People really did lash out against this mayor, saying that he just didn't care at all about the city, and certainly not at all about black people."

Robertson did somewhat exonerate the late mayor in her remarks, suggesting that his position may have been grounded in his inherent obstinacy more than a basic racism. "But as a child, all I could think was, he is so low-down!"

I spoke about Mayor Henry Loeb, who died in 1992, with his son Henry G. Loeb Jr. Loeb still lives in Memphis and is a gregarious, open, and voluble individual in his fifties. He is not defensive about his father (many older Memphians are) but is not without his loyalties and certainties. He said upfront: "Dr. King was perhaps the greatest civil right proponent of modern time. Dad was crestfallen that he died in Memphis on Dad's watch. Although Dad never hypothecated any 'if I had done this then maybe that.'"

But then Henry Loeb Jr. went on the record with these comments:

> [His] character common denominators from his three elected terms were intense focus, unbending nature about his rules and regulations as to how he carried out responsibilities of elected office, and a personal mindset of acceptance of constituency trust to represent the best interests of Memphis.
>
> Despite nonfactual statements still periodically made by former MLK attorneys (one should simply read the law), the Tennessee laws regarding government employees involved in public safety or health matters NOT having a right to strike have been strengthened rather than repealed since 1968. A major issue this year [2010] in Memphis has been the present mayor trying to privatize the sanitation department for cost and service quality considerations. Of course again union leadership is crying foul play. I guess as time goes on we hopefully recognize what we have learned but we continue to demand what we expect and enact.

There is a legal rationality to this understandable defense of a father's intractability to which even a Beverly Robertson will accede during a pleasant interview in her office at the National Civil Rights Museum. But there is a greater emotional logic, perhaps, to an anecdote that she shared about a black high school boy—her future husband—and what he experienced just two days after King's murder there in Memphis.

"My future husband was going to an all-boys Catholic school, where there were very few African American boys. He was in a classroom, and they were talking about what had happened, that King got killed. So one white boy got up, and he said, 'Well he got what he deserved, yeah, he got shot, he got killed, he deserved it!' And my husband said that one of his friends got up from his seat and walked up to the guy and just knocked him out. And you know what? He and the guy just walked out and went to the office. And when they went to the office, the principal looked at them and said, 'I understand. Go home. I understand.' But that was so painful for those two black boys because that came from home. That had to have come from home. That had to come from conversations around the dinner table and in the house."

Robertson then pointed out that the museum had just that week hosted a conference about immigration history. "What an opportunity," she said at first, with a trace of irony. "And it was a great event and so appropriate for this place. And there were so many cultures that came. They came and they were in the auditorium, and there was a lot of learning. And the newspaper covered it. The *Commercial Appeal.* But you wouldn't believe the blogs that began to appear: 'Oh yeah, there they go again, the National Civil Rights Museum, those damn Marxists trying to stain our country. You all just trying to indoctrinate them. You all need to be just shut down.' You wouldn't believe. Now it's not all white people doing that kind of thing, of course not. And a lot of that stuff comes from right across there in Mississippi. They hold these notions. But we're not trying to say that white people are low-down dirty and wrong. That's not what this is designed to do. This is about an important segment of American history. And not all history is beautiful."

If history were beautiful, Billy Kyles wouldn't be walking the world telling a story that won't loosen its grip off his soul, Martin Luther King Jr. would be a grandfather, and Beverly Robertson wouldn't be glancing up at a bloodstained balcony every day on her way into work.

CHAPTER TWELVE

Producing *The Witness* at the Lorraine: Margaret Hyde

t's not likely that Rev. Martin Luther King Jr. and the glittering red carpet at the annual Academy Awards in Hollywood are generally associated in the same thought. King did proudly don a tuxedo for his acceptance of the 1964 Nobel Peace Prize in Oslo, Norway—an occasion of significant pageantry. He was there, however, for his cumulative work (and frequent imprisonments) in the name of human rights; what specifically garnered him the designation as a laureate was his now classic letter from the Birmingham city jail, which he penned on torn and tattered pieces of paper that were passed to him by his attorneys. The eloquence of this letter, in which King expressed his moral outrage with the clergy of Birmingham, who more or less wanted him to quit the city and stop stirring the pot of protest, has landed the document onto the short list of the greatest freedom writs of all time.

But King never went to Hollywood or sought that kind of limelight. Indeed, when people like Harry Belafonte were seen with King, it would be along the highway between Selma and Montgomery, Alabama, taking part in a rigorous and potentially dangerous foot march for voting rights. Belafonte was among several Hollywood celebrities who helped MLK physically and financially, and they went to him much more often than he went to them.

But that was a long time ago, and those were the tasks that lay at the hands of the people who believed that human dignity was at the core of American values, regardless of the skin color of the American in question. Now, more than a generation and a half later, with the world still brimming with racial and tribal wars, with religiously driven terrorism, with radical theologies pervading so many national political discussions, with Americans wringing their hands defensively about "protecting our borders" and "rounding up illegals," all while we have been burning Iraq and Afghanistan without any clear resolution or consensus since the early 1990s, we long for the clarion recollection of moral and clear-eyed leadership.

John F. Kennedy remains the hagiographic prototype of the champion president, and we elected Barack Obama because, at the time, he appeared to be the living reembodiment of Martin Luther King and Robert F. Kennedy.

And so a young white woman who reminds me "I wasn't alive when Dr. King was here" appeared on the red carpet at the 2009 Academy Awards. Margaret Hyde, in her thirties, a mother, international travel photographer, children's author, conservationist, and filmmaker, was being interviewed live standing next to Rev. Billy Kyles, the featured subject of Hyde's film *The Witness: From the Balcony of Room 306*. Also present was the film's director, Adam Pertofsky. The three of them were being cheerfully questioned by the requisite male/female anchors of TV Guide Network because *The Witness* had received an Oscar nomination for Best Documentary—Short Subject.

Kyles was particularly suave in his crisp formal ensemble, greeting the microphone-carrying emcees with a smooth, "How are you?" and doing much of the reminiscing. "It was a labor of love," he said, deeply satisfied and expressing almost a reluctance to have been involved in the project. "She"—referring to Hyde—"got on me for years to do it."

Evidently, Kyles had not spoken very much publicly about his story during the initial years after the assassination. This was Margaret Hyde's strong assertion to me when we met in her Santa Monica, California, home in the fall of 2010. In fact, we all have a harvest of stories and testimonials on the record due, again, to the quiet efforts of her father, J. R. "Pitt" Hyde, who engaged his then-teenage daughter in a museum-related video project in the early 1990s.

"Many, many people from the movement came back to Memphis for the opening of the museum. Some were people you have heard of, some were not. My dad hired a film crew to record the stories of these many ordinary people who were returning who had been a part of the history. For the months of July and August [1991] I heard countless stories, and they were all moving and all unique, and I got a sense of how many people were truly affected by the movement. And how many people it took to become 'sick and tired of being sick and tired.' These were doctors and lawyers and garbage workers and maids and moms just doing what they thought needed to be done."

Hyde recalled the opening of the museum and being able to tour the facility with the likes of Benjamin Hooks, Rosa Parks, Maxine Smith, and, of course, Billy Kyles. It was at that time, in that environment of recollection, she says, that Kyles first began relating the story of his arrival to collect King for dinner on April 4, 1968, and the subsequent moment of the assassination on the balcony outside Room 306.

Margaret Hyde recalls many other people, whose names are not recognized, suddenly bursting with personal stories of pain, difficulty, and occasional triumph, in corresponding sections of the museum that related to their experiences. "I was blown away," she said. "I really hadn't learned any of this in school yet had enjoyed the benefit of a superior education in Memphis. This wasn't in the textbooks, and the one thing I will say is that I learned very little about the civil rights movement. And it's still like a blip in the textbooks, unless individual teachers address it. Frankly, while growing up, I didn't even know the Lorraine Motel was there."

I had heard this before—and frequently. Betty Ann Hoehn, a writer and art educator who grew up similarly privileged in Memphis society with two protective brothers, gilded parents, and a nanny about whom she has written a genuinely affectionate memoir, tells me: "The Lorraine Motel was about as far away from my world as anything could be." Betty Ann recalls the cold indifference and even the grisly satisfaction expressed by her female classmates in her private school when news came of the King assassination. In her case, thanks to the humanizing and eye-opening presence of her nanny, she became so appalled that she would literally flee Memphis via college in Maine and ultimately settle in California. It must be noted that she was plenty shocked by the shoddy racial attitudes she discovered on both coasts as well; Memphis does not exist in a vacuum of social values.

Meanwhile, Margaret Hyde emphasizes the tremendous socioeconomic setback suffered by Memphis, and the inherent unfairness of the fact that, in the aftermath of the King assassination, "Memphis got blamed even though, in my opinion, it had nothing to do with Memphis. He [the assassin] was following Dr. King. It could have happened in Atlanta, it could have happened in L.A. It happens that he had the easiest shot in Memphis. Memphis got blamed and people boycotted Memphis, and it was considered a blight on the city."

"Your father called it a 'black eye on the city,'" I remarked.

"Yeah. And Memphis went into a recession, depression, especially the downtown area when other cities were still booming. Ironically, that saved some of the old buildings. My Dad feels that is why you don't see a lot of those bad '60s- and '70s-style buildings in downtown. But the bottom line is, no one really wanted to talk about it, and it was looked at as a kind of embarrassment. And that is where some of the controversy arose concerning the Lorraine Motel. There were a lot of people who saw it as a place that just needed to be wiped off the face of the earth. Get rid of it. It's the most embarrassing thing of all. But in fact, it's such a powerful place, it's something that needed to be preserved, and I'm really grateful to all the people you met who felt that way." Margaret paused. "Because it was a long battle." She let out a chuckle that betrayed more knowing anguish than hilarity.

Margaret conveyed that one of the key reasons she was motivated to make *The Witness* had to do with the courageous pluck of the Memphis sanitation workers and their unforgettable I AM A MAN mantra of the spring of 1968. "Dr. King died coming to get them a ten-cent raise," she said. "This is one thing young people really take away from the film. It, like, blows their minds. You see, I learned very little of this because people just wanted to sweep it under the rug.

"When I heard all these stories told by all these people, I was incredibly moved. I didn't know at the time what I could do about it or what it would mean to me. But as the years went by, and I continued to hear Rev. Kyles tell the story to countless winners of the Freedom Award, dignitaries, former presidents, and it would make these people cry and move them, I knew that everyone needed to hear it. And he wasn't going to be alive long enough for everybody to hear it."

Margaret returns to Memphis annually for the Freedom Award festivities. She related that one year, Kyles was absent from the event due to a surgery from which he was recovering. And although other notables whom she admires led the tour of the museum and shared their narratives, the absence of Kyles was harsh and distressing—it just wasn't the same. Within a year, and with the fortieth anniversary of the King assassination looming in 2008, she finally persuaded Billy Kyles to participate in a documentary. Through her father, she also gained the family's foundation's support as well as that of the other donors—"It was all made with nonprofit money"—and what would become an HBO-featured, Emmy- and Oscar-nominated feature began to be realized.

In addition to Kyles, the film features a number of interviews with Maxine Smith, with whom Margaret is also very close, and the lionlike Ben Hooks, who died in April 2010. Margaret wanted to include Maxine's husband, Vasco, deceased in 2009—given that the husband and wife were inseparable partners in the civil rights struggle for some fifty years. Vasco quietly declined, Hyde said. "He told me to let Maxine go on. He said, 'I liked Dr. King so much. But I cherished the fight itself. This is not for me.'"

· · · · ·

Margaret told me, "I was raised, really, by an African American woman who I called my Mama Chris. This sounds all weird and 'Gone with the Wind,' but I adored her and I supported her until she died. She was a wonderful woman. There was a real conflict for me, I could never accept the racist things I would hear, certainly not from my parents, but there was still pervasive, sort of unspoken segregation and racism. Those things didn't jive with the quality of the person that I had in my home every day. From a starting place, I think that this changed my perspective on all this. This was fundamental to me really, recognizing the damage done by racism and also that African American people are people. There is no difference. Because that's what racist people try to do, define the differences. This wouldn't work for me even as a kid."

Hyde links her childhood experience with Mama Chris—who minded her, fed her, listened to her secrets and dreams even as her two very busy parents tended to careers, businesses, projects, and considerable philanthropy—to "the privilege" of then hearing "the stories" and knowing people like Billy Kyles and so many other African Americans who lived through the real nuts and bolts of the civil rights movement. The result is a young woman blessed with great talents and resources essentially turning both over to the twenty-first-century chronicling of the twentieth-century American freedom saga. This she does with art, photography, text, and filmmaking—and a desire for her own children to learn the language of tolerance through stories.

"When you meet people who have walked this walk, who are so intelligent, who have been through so much, yet are still incredibly gracious, totally still willing to embrace you, regardless of the color of your skin . . . I mean, that is what the movement was all about. They really lived that."

"You didn't have to care about these things, Margaret," I offered.

"No, but I think when you were exposed the way I was to other people's races and cultures, when you saw that someone who raised you wasn't being treated the way you were, it's harder for those things to be okay."

CHAPTER THIRTEEN

Room 306 and Today's Young Artists: Craig Alan Edwards and Katori Hall

I n the simple, almost transient-looking one-story space called Cypress Hall D, set among more marble and architecturally appealing buildings on the campus of Stanford University, sits the Dr. Martin Luther King, Jr. Research and Education Institute. Here is housed the world's most complete collection of the reverend's speeches, letters, papers, and published and unpublished works, as well as an ongoing documentation and collection of his life's work in text, microfilm, and video.

In one of the hallway display cases, almost lost among the strata of clippings, photographs, old programs, book covers, and assorted magazine flaps, a familiar face and a well-known number jump out at this observer: Craig Alan Edwards, a well-built, doe-eyed, young African American man, dressed as and startlingly resembling Martin Luther King Jr., stands in a white shirt and tie, holding his dark sports coat just outside the blue door of

Room 306 and the white-curtained double windows. His left hand straddles the blue-painted balcony railing.

One is viewing the *New York Times* review, dated January 27, 2010, of Edwards's one-man play (which he wrote and starred in) called *The Man in Room 306*. The favorable notice, now one of thousands of archival items at the MLK institute headed by Clayborne Carson, was written by Rachel Saltz, and includes this summary:

> Dr. King fantasizes about what it would have been like to be a star ballplayer or an opera singer, tries to write a speech but reads the sports page instead, and looks back at his career, family and peccadilloes.
>
> Mr. Edwards also gives us the Dr. King whose moral imagination fueled a movement, the prince (like Buddha as much as Gandhi) who has become a radical egalitarian. Overworked and running on too little sleep, this Dr. King is increasingly under siege. Black power threatens his project of nonviolence. And the F.B.I. watches and listens wherever he goes: Is that a bug in his cigarette lighter? It is.
>
> His life, as he takes stock, has become a series of hotel rooms like this one, with its overflowing ashtray, plate of cold food and, for company, the telephone, radio and television.

"One of the more motivating aspects of the play," Edwards told me in the fall of 2010, "was the set." Indeed, the *New York Times* noted that the small theater had been converted into a replica of the Lorraine Motel, complete with the well-known neon motel sign in the background. Every audience member had to "step onto the infamous motel balcony before entering the room itself," the paper reported, and thus was "challenged to confront viscerally one of the most tragic moments in our country's history: the assassination of the Rev. Dr. Martin Luther King Jr. on April 4, 1968."

Craig Alan Edwards is an actor, and he is constantly looking for work, but he is too young to have any personal recollection of King or the preacher's times. He was born in Orange County, California, a bastion of political conservatism, though he did grow up in Philadelphia. He wants to make it in movies, like almost any red-blooded performing artist. He checks the classifieds in *Backstage* and struggles with bouts of depression during those long periods of thin working opportunities in New York that are known by most of the thousands of dreaming actors that adorn the city with energy and flair and wistfulness day in and day out.

Yet Edwards has a piece of MLK in his soul that is uncommon, deep, and directly associated with Room 306 of the Lorraine Motel. This signal, this stimulus from the spirit of King, may lie deeper within Edwards than the young man's natural desire to perform before an audience. "A long time ago," he said, "I looked over some of the Ernest Withers photographs. I saw something in the man, in King, that came out at me. Here is a man, like so many great men and women, who could have made millions of dollars with those natural talents and skills, with his oratory and scholarship, and instead went into the service of humanity. You know, he never had much money at all. There just aren't many truly great ones in our generation, in our times. They are all so homogenized, and some of them even try to steal the mantle of Dr. King while taking in millions. Look at Glenn Beck, for example."

Neither one of us, me fairly older than Craig, wanted to take a look at Glenn Beck. But we did share the longing at that moment for that fleeting greatness Edwards described. "I love the craft of the tongue and the word," said the playwright, who early on staged his *The Man in Room 306* in Memphis—in association with the National Civil Rights Museum. It opened at the Memphis Repertory Theater in 2000, and the "hands-on" set was designed by the same museum personnel who had reconstructed the original Room 306 at the Lorraine for the museum. Beverly Robertson, who expresses a great fondness for Edwards, remembers that the museum also set up a commissioned set of Ernest Withers photographs in the theater lobby to coincide with the run.

"I actually met Mr. Withers," Edwards told me, his voice quivering with excitement. "What an unbelievable thing. All these civil rights icons and these photographs all converging around this play I wrote, and me with the honor of performing as Dr. King in their midst!" He conveyed with considerable pride that because of the nature of the set construction, the audience literally walks across "the balcony" past the window of Room 306 and into the space of the room, where they sit and watch. "They see and hear it just the way it was. There is the *TV Guide* with Lucille Ball on the cover. It's all about the voices and music of 1968. We ran tapes of original broadcasts from WDIA."

In January 2000 the *American Theater* magazine reported from Memphis that Edwards had "become obsessed with King's voice after rummaging through recordings of old speeches in the library" of Boston University. Craig told me, "I was really overwhelmed by his brilliance and by the passionate idealism. I could not get enough of the sound of his voice." Indeed, theater critics and audience members have been struck, even moved, by Craig's remarkable acquisition of the preacher's fabled cadence and delivery—although the play takes place before the "Mountaintop" preachment and within the privacy and seclusion of Room 306.

Edwards was motivated to make what he terms "a pilgrimage" to the Lorraine Motel, where the script and the story began to be realized in his head. *American Theater* noted: "He chose Room 306 as the site of his play. In this musty motel setting, we see King prepare notes for what will be his legendary last speech [the 'Mountaintop']. A half-eaten tray of food, scattered copies of *Life* magazine, empty bottles of Coke litter the scene, and a cigarette hangs from the corner of this mouth—certainly not an image popularly associated with the revered civil rights leader."

Never mind that in reality, Martin Luther King never formally prepared for the "Mountaintop" speech. In the dark prophecy of his death that closed the speech was its mysticism. After all, he had all but turned down for the evening in Room 306 and commissioned Ralph Abernathy to speak in his stead at Mason Temple that stormy Wednesday night. Ralph's call from Mason ("They want you, Martin") created the scenario for one of the most memorable and spontaneous moments of divination in modern history. Nonetheless, to borrow from MLK's own words that night, "But it doesn't really matter now." Craig Alan Edwards, in bringing art to history, tells me, "I just want to humanize the man. He was real, three-dimensional. He was not just an icon or a symbol."

Certainly, the many people who actually rubbed shoulders with King in and around the Lorraine Motel, from the sons of Ernest Withers to Georgia Davis Powers to Billy Kyles to Charles Newman, have concurred that he was a real person with every dimension.

$$\cdots\cdots$$

Cheryl Katz, who has directed *The Man in Room 306* and has been with Edwards and the production for more than ten years and its incarnations in Memphis, New Jersey, and New York, spoke to me about the experience. Katz is director of play development at Luna Stage in West Orange, New Jersey. She recalled that in 2000, when she and Edwards and the production company appeared in Memphis, Beverly Robertson and the entire museum staff were "incredibly supportive." She added, "Like you, they recognize in Craig that this is not a person who is looking for an opportunity to just ride the coattails of Dr. King. But he is looking to continue his message and continue his work. They were taken and moved by Craig's authenticity, as a person and as an artist and as a historian. But Craig's mission could only take place at the Lorraine Motel."

The museum staff escorted the artists through a private tour of the exhibits and gave them access to the Withers photograph collection. Like Craig, Cheryl also hailed the meeting that occurred with the iconic photographer. "He was to be called 'Mr. Withers,'" she emphasized. "These included archival photos of the Lorraine Motel itself, so we were able to get a better idea of how to build our set and literally transport the audience back to that time and place."

What was it like for this imaginative woman from Philadelphia, a professional versed in dramaturgy much more than southern history, to venture down to Memphis and stage this production about Martin Luther King?

"Going to Memphis," she told me, "was truly powerful. Memphis is a haunting city, you can feel the ghosts." Katz shared that after one particular performance of *The Man in Room 306* in New York in 2010, as she and Edwards awaited the response of the critics, she was overwhelmed by a memory of being in Memphis.

"I actually said to Craig, 'Who cares what they say here about it? They liked it in Memphis. It's what they felt in Memphis that matters.' Memphis is where it happened. Memphis is where people who experienced it actually came to see the production. It's in that experience that art is redeemed, that it has value."

Katz recalled that one evening, after a staging in Memphis, a middle-aged woman pulled her aside. The woman was emotional and told Katz that as a young girl, she was supposed to have gone to the sanitation workers' march with King (on March 28, 1968) that was overrun by the Invaders and perhaps other agitators and ended in broken glass and blood. The woman's mother forbade her from attending, fearing exactly the kind of violence that broke up the protest and sent King in doleful retreat to the Rivermont Motel.

"This woman had all her life been tethered to this moment in time," said Katz. "She told me how moved she was by the production and how it took her back to this moment, and it was healing for her. I will never forget that woman. And you just don't get a higher approval of your work than from something like that."

· · · · ·

Thirty-year-old Katori Hall, an actress and prizewinning playwright and native of Memphis, returned to her hometown in the spring of 2010. She was photographed under vivid sunshine outside the wreathed balcony of the former Lorraine Motel at the National Civil Rights Museum. Her strong, comely facial features and deep, thinking eyes revealed her powerful spiritual relationship to the place; she had just become the first black woman to receive the Laurence Olivier Award in London for her original play, *The Mountaintop.*

· · · · ·

The play is a speculation about King's final night in Room 306—after he returns from Mason Temple and the delivery of his "Mountaintop" speech. Like Craig Alan Edwards, Hall also gives us a significantly humanized MLK, a complex and driven man troubled by demons, loneliness, conflicted feelings about his vaunted world status, and certainly his libido. Hall's two–person drama, involving only King and a fictional Lorraine maid named Camae, captivated British audiences and was the upstart winner of the Olivier Award—the West End equivalent of the Tony Award for Best Play.

Journalist Christopher Blank, who filed an interview with Hall for the *Memphis Commercial Appeal*, reported that the play was bound for Broadway; indeed, it had been cast with Samuel L. Jackson as King and Angela Bassett as Camae and, after a delay, was scheduled to open in New York in the fall of 2011.

In London, theater critic Nicola Christie had written the following about the production by the young woman from Memphis who was born thirteen years after King's murder at the Lorraine Motel:

> One minute the pastor and his new friend are beating each other up with rounds of oratory; the next, they're trying out how to look sexy while smoking. We discover, too, that King has stinky feet, wonders whether his moustache looks good on him or not and has an eye for the ladies. We also learn that he is terrified. Terrified that he is about to die, that the attempts on his life will finally get him. Terrified that he hasn't had the chance to fix the world and that he hasn't said good-bye to his wife and children.

Katori Hall attended Craigmont High School in Memphis before going off to Columbia University, Harvard, and Julliard. Classmates and teachers alike in Memphis knew that she was a wunderkind. She would apply the poignancy and melancholy of southern history, of Memphis neighborhoods such as the aptly named Hurt Village, into living American literature.

"I remember her so well," Otis Sanford told me. The great columnist and managing editor of the *Commercial Appeal* for thirty-five years beamed when we spoke about Katori Hall. "Yes, she was a big part of the *Teen Appeal*, a citywide newspaper I started for the Memphis high schools back in 1997. She is a wonderful person."

And what if, one thinks, Chuck Scruggs had not made his appeals from radio station WDIA to help Walter Bailey save his forlorn and bloodied motel in the aftermath of April 4, 1968? What if D'Army Bailey hadn't run into Walter Bailey on a Memphis street corner some years later and made up his mind to do something about making the Lorraine not disappear? What if Pitt Hyde had not put up with years and years of intra–African American bickering and posturing at the original museum executive committee meetings and simply walked away with his heart and his money? What if the Lorraine Motel had actually been done away with by the rapacious wrecking ball? What if King and the bloodstains and the memories and everything were simply turned to dust at Main and Mulberry?

What, then, would two young artists such as Craig Alan Edwards and Katori Hall be thinking about if Room 306 were but a rumor?

CHAPTER FOURTEEN

They Got It Done: Clayborne Carson

"We've had Billy Kyles out here a number of times," said the tall, lanky scholar who sat comfortably across from me. Clayborne Carson, historian, researcher, and international lecturer on peace, reconciliation, and nonbelligerent protest, had received me in his office. "Kyles tells his story with power. He's really very good."

Carson has been the director of the Martin Luther King, Jr. Research and Education Institute located on the campus of Stanford University since 1985. He is informal, quiet in his speech, and more often than not can be found comfortably dressed in one of his trademark woolen sweaters of soft colors that match his trimmed white beard and thick head of hair.

He did not go seeking out the stewardship of Martin Luther King's papers and the subsequent publication and editing of copious books, anthologies, and even the Martin Luther King encyclopedia—now available on the Internet.

"Coretta called me in 1985 and asked me to do it," he told me. He finds that paradoxical, given his youthful roots in the Student Nonviolent Coordinating Committee (SNCC) and his mentors, such as Julian Bond and particularly Robert Moses.

"SNCC was in some ways opposed to Dr. King, and was committed to bottom-up, grassroots leadership, whereas King was the epitome of top-down leadership," Carson said. But before he was anything else, Clayborne Carson was a bona fide scholar, chronicler, author, and playwright with a doctorate from the University of California at Los Angeles and a multiplicity of research credentials. So he responded to Coretta Scott King's request unequivocally and has become the embodiment of the institute. A senior adviser to the *Eyes on the Prize* series, he has examined apartheid in South Africa, explored Gandhian philosophy in India, and served as a consultant to the architectural team that created the National Civil Rights Museum.

Clay Carson, though carrying the burden of the King Papers Project for some twenty-five years, along with the attendant weightiness of endless documents, data, and media, as well as the singular responsibility of looking after the papers and documents of Martin Luther King, nonetheless is light on his feet. His expression is a blend of interest and kindness. He is like a pleasantly dressed version of Gandhi who drives a late-model Acura but could be easily perceived as spindling yarn and talking of *ahisma* (total nonviolence) just as the Mahatma did.

Carson knows about everything related to MLK and the movement, from the 1955 Montgomery bus boycott to the 1963 March on Washington (which he attended as a nineteen-year-old) to the Birmingham Sixteenth Street church bombing that killed four little girls to Selma's "Bloody Sunday" in 1965 to the storyline of the Lorraine Motel.

I went to see Carson, some 2,000 miles from Memphis, within the airy realm of the Bay Area, just about as far as one can get from Beale Street and barbecue ribs, to gain a perspective on the Lorraine Motel, history, and significance.

Carson mentioned Rev. Jim Lawson's nagging doubts about the true story of what occurred on April 4, 1968, at the Lorraine Motel. "Doesn't he still believe that Dr. King's presence in Room 306, given its openness and visibility, was not accidental?" Yes, he does believe this, we agreed. "Because when you think back," continued Carson, perhaps of similar mind, "306 was not a well-placed room, and any security personnel would have said 'no, you can't stay there.'"

Then Carson asked me, "Is the woman who protests still out there?"

The reference was to the somewhat infamous Jacqueline Smith, who has maintained a vigil and a filibuster-style protest just outside the National Civil Rights Museum for over fifteen years, as well as a "Fulfill the Dream" website. She wants to spearhead a boycott of the museum. D'Army Bailey, not surprisingly, is a fan and supporter of Smith, who was apparently the last tenant in the Lorraine Motel, stayed on after the MLK assassination, and was finally evicted. Smith fervently believes that the subsequent museum is unfitting and racist and an accessory vehicle to the gentrification of the area—at the expense of poor people like herself who were removed in order to make way for the project.

When I spoke to Smith once, in her tent display showcase next to the museum grounds, she was wearing all-dark clothes and a black scarf. She is articulate, appears younger than her years, and is expressive. There is a distinct edginess to her. She stubbornly remained in her room at the Lorraine until the purchase of the property by the Martin Luther King Jr. Memorial Foundation in 1982. She has placards, statements, endorsements, flyers, photos, memorial flowerpots, and a well-endowed donations box. Whatever her motives, she is tethered to the site and vehemently objects to "the corporate culture" that has replaced what was home to a number of impoverished Memphis folks. "I am here in the true spirit of Dr. King," she told me, "and the Poor People's Campaign he was mobilizing when he was killed here in 1968." *Time* magazine offered a feature about the obdurate and feisty Smith in 1990, noting that "she thinks the place should be used to house the homeless in tribute to King."

I suggested to Carson that even the obsession (or ostentation) of a Jacqueline Smith in the matter of the museum could be a backhanded tribute to its undeniably high profile as a national freedom tabernacle. Could it be, given the Lorraine, given the many historic personalities who have resided and campaigned in Memphis, that the city has more of a centrality in the civil rights movement than even Atlanta and its MLK center governed by the King family?

"Certainly," responded Carson, "given what has happened in Atlanta with the National Park Service, you don't really have much of a facility there other than the Visitor Center, and, of course the graves of Martin and Coretta King." Carson was referring to the fact that in 1980, the Park Service took over the center and its environs and established the Martin Luther King Historic Site. The district includes the Center for Nonviolent Social Change originally established by Mrs. King, the Ebenezer Baptist Church, MLK's nearby birth home, and the immediate area of "Sweet Auburn" Avenue and adjacent streets. The Park Service's jurisdiction over the area, originally agreed to by the King family, has led to restricted hours for visiting and created some expansion difficulties. Moreover, the King children have, sadly enough, often been at odds with each other over a number of matters related to King's legacy. They retain the actual King Visitor Center as an "inholding" and continue to battle with each other and with the government over whether to sell the spot to the National Park Service.

"The Visitor Center hasn't been updated for over twenty years," said Carson. "My voice is still there on a recording for visitors, and that hasn't been changed in twenty years." A sadness briefly hung over the modest office filled with books, photos of Gandhi and King, and mementos of Carson's many visits to India, China, South Africa, Zimbabwe, Tanzania, England, France, Germany, Holland, Belgium, Israel, and the Palestinian territories.

But for the phone call from Coretta Scott King in 1985, asking him to edit the King papers, "I would not be doing this work," Carson said. He again emphasized the irony—when he appeared at the 1963 March on Washington, he hooked up with more radical types, "the critics of King," such as Stokely Carmichael and Bob Moses and other leaders of SNCC. "But Mrs. King likely recognized my overall interest in the history of the movement, and I do see that as my mission. But King, of course, is the symbol of the movement."

A number of circumstances led Carson to the Lorraine Motel over the years. "I consulted with the design firm that actually created some of their exhibits. I worked with them on the main center and then the expansion." Yes, he met D'Army Bailey in the course of his consultancies, and certainly spoke often with Pitt Hyde.

"It was very political," he said, "with Bailey using the desire of Memphis and the state of Tennessee to redevelop the central area. They had to get the money and the incentive to involve the business community. It worked. It meant certain compromises along the way, but politics is a messy business. It's the same kind of thing they said about the health care debate we just went through. 'You don't want to see sausage being made.' There was a lot of sausage made there in Memphis. A lot of enemies were made. But they got it done. And it is the preeminent civil rights museum."

The Rain Are Fallin

There are eighteen standing exhibits in the main Lorraine building of the National Civil Rights Museum, plus a "Voices of Civil Rights" kiosk and a Mahatma Gandhi timeline and video presentation. Since 2002, eleven more exhibits appear in the "Exploring the Legacy" expansion structure just adjacent—known today as the Young and Morrow Building. This is largely the former Canipe's Amusement store and the rooming house of Bessie Brewer, from where the assassin, standing in the stained and rusty community bathtub, peered out the window at the Lorraine balcony and suddenly discovered the target he had been stalking for months and across the nation. The "Legacy" exhibition, largely underwritten by the Hyde Family Foundation, also includes a permanent installation of the Ernest C. Withers's I AM A MAN portfolio.

This secondary exhibition, besides containing a replica 1966 Ford Mustang automobile and other items associated with the accused killer, James Earl Ray, has another unique distinction: the museum became official custodian of the police and evidence files associated with the manhunt, indictment, and confession of James Earl Ray. As a result, the museum has become the first of its kind to receive legal and forensic materials and court documents connected with a criminal case into its collection holdings.

Retired congressman Louis Stokes, a longtime friend of the author, was for decades the only African American member from Ohio serving in the U.S. House of Representatives. Besides chairing the Congressional Black Caucus, Stokes also headed the House Select Committee on Assassinations in the mid-1970s, which revisited the investigations of both the assassinations of President John F. Kennedy and Martin Luther King Jr. Stokes told me that he personally interviewed James Earl Ray and that his committee (which left the door open to conspiracy theories in both cases) visited and surveyed the site of the MLK assassination—or, as it turned out, a segment of it.

"I looked out the window that the suspect was supposed to have used for the shooting," said Stokes. "Yes, the Lorraine balcony was very much in plain sight, very close." At the time of the committee members' official visit, the Lorraine was moldering in what Andrew Withers had described to me as the "absentee" period. There was no museum, no unfettered access to the balcony itself without the possible interference of prostitutes, vagrants, and the general seediness of the neighborhood. Somewhat to my surprise, Stokes told me that, no, he did not have a recollection of actually alighting on the motel area itself—it was not part of the explicit issue of his committee's work on that occasion. The committee was studying the assassin, access, trajectory, and the like. I know in my heart, however, that Louis Stokes, whose brother Carl was elected the first African American mayor of a major U.S. city in 1967 (Cleveland), would have assuredly walked over if the site were already the National Civil Rights Museum.

Meanwhile, my friend remains circumspect about the case and his own views on what happened that evening of April 4, 1968.

So now, though most visitors think of the former Lorraine building as the museum locale, the expansion is very much part of "the collection." The gross square footage of the museum is 47,303, and it occupies 4.14 acres of land. Once they have paid admission fees or joined the museum, people may move about at their leisure throughout the site. The balcony outside Room 306 is not open to the public and is visited by special arrangement and with escort only. Attendance at the museum has steadily risen annually over the years, a testament to its leadership, its value, and the unremitting attachment of the American and global community to Martin Luther King.

· · · · ·

Amanda Woods, an Australian travel journalist, came to explore Memphis in 2009. She initially thought of the museum as one of the city's many prominent tourist attractions, along with the Elvis Presley mansion, St. Jude Hospital, Beale Street, Peabody Place, and the Rock 'n' Soul Museum. She was overcome with emotion at the Lorraine, and wrote, simply: "Elvis Presley's Graceland may be the best known tourist attraction in Memphis, but the National Civil Rights Museum is the most powerful."

In the spring of 2007, just days before both the start of the season and the thirty-ninth anniversary of the MLK assassination, Major League Baseball inaugurated its annual Civil Rights Game. The game was played in Memphis, at the ballpark named for Pitt Hyde's Auto Zone Company. A classic Memphis rain drenched the field and canceled batting practice for both the St. Louis Cardinals and the Cleveland Indians, yet the skies cleared in time for Patti LaBelle to offer up a heart-throbbing rendition of "The Star Spangled Banner" and for Benjamin Hooks to throw out the ceremonial first pitch. Later, during the "seventh-inning stretch," the Civil Rights Museum Choir sang "America, the Beautiful."

C. C. Sabathia and his Cleveland teammates had come to the ballpark following an extended private tour of the museum that Saturday. Sabathia, a husky, accomplished, rising star of a pitcher (who soon enough wound up with the New York Yankees), was all but overwhelmed by the experience. On that day he was not so much a baseball luminary as he was a young black man coming to terms with the reality of history. He told reporters, quietly: "It was humbling. It was definitely humbling. I don't know what else to say."

Sabathia, good-natured, known for his charitable inclinations, was also quoted as saying: "The whole thing was kind of surreal. It was weird, it was eerie—very eerie, you know." Evidently, the young man was very affected by the exhibited history of segregation, lynching, and visceral racism built into American culture—including the baseball culture, until the emergence of Jackie Robinson in 1947 (though Robinson's physical entry onto the playing field hardly eviscerated the racial ugliness that pervaded the game for some time).

MLB.com reported: "[Sabathia] found he couldn't step into the motel portion of the exhibition. He took a glance at it; he wanted to go inside, he said. He simply couldn't will himself to take those steps. Perhaps the pain of walking where a civil rights icon had lost his life proved too much for Sabathia." The pitcher related that he called his wife and bade her to come back with him, along with their young son, as soon as the boy was old enough to understand what he would see at the museum. "Touring that museum would definitely humble a lot of people," said Sabathia, as he sat by his locker at the ball park, somewhat alone with his thoughts but for the hovering journalists.

A year later the New York Mets came to Memphis for the Civil Rights Game to play the Florida Marlins. The bench coach and future manager of the Mets was Jerry Manuel—"the Sage," as he was called. Born in Hariha, Georgia, in 1953, Manuel has borne a lifetime reverence for Martin Luther King. While he was thrilled to be a part of the second Civil Rights Game, Manuel was focused on one thing: getting himself and his young protégés to the National Civil Rights Museum. Manuel told the *New York Daily News*: "To go there with the team was big. Personally, I'm glad I went with the team because if I didn't, I'd probably still be there going through the stuff. It was emotional for me because Martin Luther King was a hero for me. It was huge. Huge."

Subsequent Civil Rights games have been played in Cincinnati, with a linkage to its National Underground Railroad Museum and Freedom Center, and in Atlanta, with its obvious roots to the civil rights movement and the King family. Jimmie Lee Solomon, executive vice president of Major League

Baseball, told me: "We want other cities with the history to be represented via the game." Nonetheless, Major League Baseball anointed Memphis as the provenance of the Civil Rights Game, and the museum as part of the proceedings.

· · · · ·

Yes, it is a perennial civil rights magnet, and the emergent museum, raised from gore and dust, is at its historical center. The once-drab motel of my historical fantasies does exist, as does the resilient city that brings three Confederate states to a bittersweet juncture of water, blood, geography, and memory. Rarely do you fly into Memphis without encountering purple mists and hovering ghosts, the plane reeling from clouds and a lingering rain. You feel MLK's sad spirit floating over the gray Mississippi River, the green landscape, and the brownish buildings below. You note the ball fields, the freeways, the strip malls that, from the clouds above, identify the city as boilerplate American.

Yet something languorous rises, like a reluctant steam, betraying this as a painfully unique southern city. The silent old elm trees hide secrets and regrets under their thick leaves. Memphis lacks the Grand Ole Opry cheek of Nashville, the sleek CNN beam of Atlanta, the steely firmness of Birmingham, the bluegrass opulence of Lexington, and it is somewhat devoid of the antebellum stillness of Tallahassee and Savannah. Yet Memphis is open to its own pain; its black soil is overgrown with forced transition, it heaves against its own melancholy, and—when the forgiving sunshine breaks through—it gleams like a boisterous, reigning corporate hub where cotton and genteelism once ruled. Memphis is as sassy as any sizzling barbecue sauce, as elegiac as the wrinkled necks of the sons of sharecroppers who still polish wood and valet at the Marriott and the Peabody and who remember the day when men lost their minds and women held their hearts and Martin Luther King Jr. lay bleeding on the balcony of Walter and Lorene's blue and yellow motel at Main and Mulberry.

In the museum, somewhere among the exhibitions about the early slave revolts of the seventeenth century, the Dred Scott case (involving a slave who unsuccessfully sued for his freedom in 1857), the 1909 founding of the NAACP, the ignominious Emmett Till saga, the savage reign of Jim Crow, the landmark *Brown v. Topeka Board of Education* ruling of 1954, the Little Rock high school diorama, the rebuilt Montgomery bus recalling the 1955 boycott, the replicated Birmingham jail cell of King as well the 1963 March on Washington podium, the Freedom Summer and Selma march panoramas, the lunch-counter sit-ins, a burned-out Greyhound Bus, and the Memphis garbage trucks, there is a singular photo. It contains no blood, no frightened faces, and no imminent sense of danger or threat.

It is a brownish, faded photograph, somewhat resembling an old daguerreotype in finish, of a one-room schoolhouse. It is the late 1940s, somewhere in the Deep South—a slender, smiling African American teacher is standing over her small cadre of black students in what is clearly an all-day classroom with inadequate supplies, broken-down desks, poor lighting, no amenities, and a single, worn blackboard hanging sideways on an obviously thin wall. There is an air of good cheer and determination, nonetheless, in the eyes of the teacher. She is pointing to the chalkboard, where she has written a phrase for her students to repeat and learn. She has printed the phrase in clear, upright letters:

THE RAIN ARE FALLIN.

Can anyone see this photograph, hanging among the other prints of chains, police, and open fire hoses; the newsreels of bigoted men and their drawn clubs; the posters of Klansmen brandishing their burning crosses; the letters of Stokely Carmichael and Julian Bond and female pioneer Dorothy Height; the recordings of the rhythmic baritones of Martin Luther King—can anyone behold this misbegotten yet painfully noble moment between a teacher using thirdhand chalk, secondhand desks, and firsthand dignity, to teach a few American children that, no matter how they may say it, the rain is meant to quench their thirst as well?

Maxine Smith reluctantly walks along her hallway of plaques, wishing she never had to have earned them; Billy Kyles tells the story again to a visiting prime minister or a school kid from Ohio; D'Army Bailey shakes his head in consternation when yet another corporate festival seems to taint the sanctity of black history as he insists upon it; Pitt Hyde remembers a paper sack of fruit he handed over to the children of sharecroppers when he chairs still another foundation grant discussion; Beverly Robertson opens her eyes in the morning and recalls the fire-engine red nail polish her father gave her even as she tries to advance yet another development graphic to help renovate the museum; Jim Lawson pulls off his glasses, shuts his eyes, and remembers the sting of Mace and holds down the tear in his throat for his long-departed Martin; Andrew and Joshua Withers think of the sizzling hot chicken and frosty soft drinks and the humming air conditioning unit at the old Lorraine grill, and the once-intractable smile of Walter Bailey under the beating Tennessee sun.

The doors of the museum open, and, as the morning air, already laden with humidity and the scent of magnolias, infiltrates and mixes in with the history and the music and the marching feet, the wreath at Room 306 bends a bit in the breeze, and another child who might not have known finds out.

Acknowledgments

The professional staff at the National Civil Rights Museum was unconditionally supportive of this project from the beginning. Beverly Robertson, president and CEO of the museum, has become a dear friend, and I am but one of innumerable writers, researchers, and artists for whom she remains a resource and ally. I am also very grateful to Barbara Andrews and Debbie Nutt, two exemplary members of the senior staff, for their guidance, wisdom, and warmth.

This book, the product of a strong personal yearning to tell this story, would have never had a chance to unfold without the constant and informative and cheerful input of Charles F. Newman of the Burch, Porter, and Johnson law firm in Memphis. Charlie, who really had a stake in the attempted legal defense of Martin Luther King Jr.'s right to march at the very end of King's life, remained approachable, generously accommodating, and kind enough to make crucial referrals.

Rev. Samuel "Billy" Kyles, my colleague and teacher, The Witness, is an inspiration to any human being who is learning to turn a tragedy into a lifelong commitment to hope. He is a man and a minister of uncommon oratorical abilities and a sweet, good soul.

Many thanks to J. R. "Pitt" Hyde and the Hyde Family Foundation for the constant graciousness and access to the personal histories that attend this narrative.

Martha Bates, my editor at Michigan State University Press, is my great champion. Jill Marr, my literary agent, is as tenderhearted as she is professionally impeccable.

It is impossible for me not to acknowledge the indomitable, clear-eyed presence and persona of Maxine Smith. I went to her home in Memphis as a journalist and left as a member of her family. Maxine's self-effacing style and her glorious wit are but the indicators of her raw courage and mighty dignity.

I am possessed of the deepest admiration for Rev. James Lawson, whose personal role in the leadership of the 1968 Memphis sanitation workers' strike and whose unyielding commitment to nonviolent, Christian protest is unmatched by any other person in this drama, and who seeks no recognition for what he did. Jim Lawson is the real thing.

I want to acknowledge the cooperation of and the use of a variety of articles and materials that have appeared in the *Memphis Commercial Appeal*, all of which are cited within the body of the work.

And to so many other participants and chroniclers of the Memphis civil rights saga, black and white, female and male, who opened their homes, their offices, and their souls to me, I express my most profound respect and gratitude.

Bibliography

Abernathy, Ralph David. *And the Walls Came Tumbling Down.* Chicago: Lawrence Hills Books, 1989.

Akers, Cissy Caldwell, et al., eds. *Lucius: Writings of Lucius Burch.* Nashville, Tenn.: Cold Tress Press, 2003.

Bailey, D'Army. *The Education of a Black Radical.* Baton Rouge: Louisiana State University Press, 2009.

———. *Mine Eyes Have Seen: Dr. Martin Luther King's Final Journey.* Memphis, Tenn.: Towery Publishing, 1993.

Beifuss, Joan. *At the River I Stand.* Memphis, Tenn.: St Lukes Press, 1990.

Branch, Taylor. *At Canaan's Edge: America in the King Years 1965–68.* New York: Simon and Schuster, 2006.

———. *Pillar of Fire: America in the King Years 1963–65.* New York: Touchstone, 1998.

Carson, Clayborne, ed. *The Autobiography of Martin Luther King.* New York: Warner Books, 1998.

Clarke, Thurston: *The Last Campaign: Robert F. Kennedy and 82 Days That Inspired America.* New York: Henry Holt, 2008.

Dyson, Michael Eric. *April 4, 1968: Martin Luther King's Death and How It Changed America.* New York: Basic Civitas Books, 2008.

———. *I May Not Get There with You: The True Martin Luther King, Jr.* New York: Touchstone, 2000.

Frady, Marshall. *Martin Luther King, Jr.* New York: Viking, 2002.

Frank, Gerold. *An American Death: The True Story of the Assassination of Martin Luther King, Jr., and the Greatest Manhunt of Our Time.* Garden City, N.Y.: Doubleday, 1972.

Garrow, David. *Bearing the Cross: Martin Luther King, Jr., and the Southern Christian Leadership Conference.* New York: William Morrow, 1986.

Halberstam, David. *The Children.* New York: Fawcett Books, 1998.

Hamill, Pete. *PieceWork: Writings on Men and Women, Fools and Heroes, Lost Cities, Vanished Friends, Small Pleasures, Large Calamities, and How the Weather Was.* Boston: Little, Brown, 1996.

Hampton, Henry, and Steve Fayer. *Voices of Freedom: An Oral History of the Civil Rights Movement from the 1950s through the 1980s.* New York: Bantam Books, 1990.

Haskins, Jim. *The Day Martin Luther King, Jr. Was Shot: A Photo History of the Civil Rights Movement.* New York: Scholastic, 1992.

Hirsch, John. *Willie Mays: The Life, the Legend.* New York: Simon and Schuster, 2010.

Honey, Michael K. *Going Down Jericho Road: The Memphis Strike, Martin Luther King's Last Campaign.* New York: W. W. Norton, 2007.

Hoppe, Sherry L., and Bruce W. Speck. *Maxine Smith's Unwilling Pupils.* Knoxville: University of Tennessee Press, 2007.

Johnson, Charles, and Bob Adelman. *King: The Photobiography of Martin Luther King, Jr.* New York: Penguin Putnam, 2000.

Kamin, Ben. *Thinking Passover: A Rabbi's Book of Holiday Values*. New York: Dutton, 1997.

Kennedy, Caroline, ed. *A Patriot's Handbook: Songs, Poems, Stories, and Speeches Celebrating the Land We Love*. New York: Hyperion, 2003.

King, Coretta Scott, ed. *The Words of Martin Luther King, Jr.* 1983. Reprint, New York: Newmarket Press, 1987.

King, Martin Luther, Jr. *Where Do We Go from Here: Chaos or Community?* Boston: Beacon Press, 1967.

Kotz, Nick. *Judgment Days: Lyndon Johnson, Martin Luther King, Jr., and the Laws That Changed America*. Boston: Houghton Mifflin, 2005.

Kurlansky, Mark. *1968: The Year That Rocked the World*. New York: Ballantine Books, 2004.

Lewis, John. *Walking with the Wind: A Memoir of the Movement*. New York: Simon and Schuster, 1998.

Manchester, William. *The Death of a President*. New York: Harper & Row, 1967.

O'Neill, William L. *Coming Apart: An Informal History of America in the 1960's*. Chicago: Quadrangle Books, 1971.

Posner, Gerald. *Killing the Dream: James Earl Ray and the Assassination of Martin Luther King, Jr.* New York: Random House, 1998.

Powers, Georgia Davis: *I Shared the Dream*. Far Hills, N.J.: New Horizon Press, 1995.

Roberts, Gene, and Hank Klibanoff. *The Race Beat: The Press, the Civil Rights Struggle, and the Awakening of a Nation*. New York: Alfred A. Knopf, 2006.

Rowan, Cart T. *Dream Makers, Dream Breakers: The World of Justice Thurgood Marshall*. Boston: Little, Brown, 1993.

Salzman, Jack, ed. *Bridges and Boundaries: African Americans and American Jews*. New York: George Braziller and The Jewish Museum, 1992.

Shatzkin, Mike, and Jim Charlton, eds. *The Ballplayers*. New York: Arbor House, 1990.

Sides, Hampton: *Hellhound on His Trail: The Stalking of Martin Luther King, Jr. and the International Hunt for His Assassin*. New York: Doubleday, 2010.

Talbot, David. *Brothers: The Hidden History of the Kennedy Years.* New York: Free Press, 2007.

Woodward, C. Vann. *The Burden of Southern History.* Baton Rouge: Louisiana State University Press, 1960.